W9-BRN-318

Bible teachers are often asked, "Which translation is the best?"

There is no simple answer. One might ask, "Best for what? For reading? For studying? For memorizing? And best for whom? For young people? For adults? For Protestants? For Catholics? For Jews?"

The author says, "My responses are not intended to be complicated; rather, they reflect the complexity of the true situation. Whereas for some language populations, there is only one translation of the Bible, English-speaking people have hundreds of translations."

Here's a book to answer your question, "What's the best translation?"

THE COMPLETE GUIDE TO

BIBLE VERSIONS

Philip Wesley Comfort
Ph.D.

LIVING BOOKS ®
Tyndale House Publishers, Inc.
Wheaton, Illinois

Scripture quotations marked KJV are taken from the *Holy Bible,* King James Version.

Scripture quotations marked RSV are taken from the *Holy Bible,* Revised Standard Version, © 1946, 1952, 1971 by the Division of Christian Education of the National Council of Churches in the United States of America.

Scripture quotations marked NRSV are taken from the *Holy Bible,* New Revised Standard Version, © 1989 by the Division of Christian Education of the National Council of Churches in the United States of America.

Scripture quotations marked NEB are taken from *The New English Bible,* © 1961, 1970 by The Delegates of the Oxford University Press and The Syndics of the Cambridge University Press.

Scripture quotations marked NASB are taken from the *New American Standard Bible,* © 1960, 1962, 1963, 1968, 1971, 1972, 1973, 1975, 1977 by The Lockman Foundation. Used by permission.

Scripture quotations marked NIV are from the *Holy Bible,* New International Version, © 1973, 1978, 1984 International Bible Society. Used by permission of Zondervan Bible Publishers.

Scripture quotations marked TEV are taken from The Good News Bible, The Bible in Today's English Version. New Testament © 1966, 1971, 1976 by the American Bible Society.

Scripture quotations marked TLB are taken from *The Living Bible,* © 1971 owned by assignment by KNT Charitable Trust. All rights reserved.

Scripture quotations marked *New American Bible* are taken from the *New American Bible,* Revised New Testament, © 1986 by the Confraternity of Christian Doctrine, Washington, D.C. All rights reserved.

Living Books is a registered trademark of Tyndale House Publishers, Inc.

Library of Congress Catalog Card Number 90-71925

ISBN 0-8423-1251-X

© 1991 by Philip W. Comfort. All rights reserved.

Chapters 7 and 8 were adapted from chapters 3 and 4 in the author's *A Study Guide to Translating the Gospel of John* (Wheaton, Ill., 1986), which has also been published in *Notes on Translation* (January 1989) as "An Analysis of Five Modern Translations of the Gospel of John."

Printed in the United States of America

97   96   95   94   93   92   91

8   7   6   5   4   3   2   1

TO MY WIFE
Georgia
WHO LIVES THE WORD

CONTENTS

INTRODUCTION

When I teach New Testament Literature and Interpretation at Wheaton College, I always give lectures about the history of the English Bible and about the various modern translations that are available to English readers. I believe it is important for students living in an age where there is a plethora of translations to know something about each one.

When I give my lectures, I am often asked, "Which translation is the best?" Invariably I respond, "Best for what? For reading? For studying? For memorizing? And best for whom? For young people? For adults? For Protestants? For Catholics? For Jews?" My responses are not intended to be complicated; rather, they reflect the complexity of the true situation. Whereas for some language populations there is only one translation of the Bible, English-speaking people have hundreds of translations.

Modern readers of the Bible, exposed to a multitude of English translations, find it difficult to determine which translation they should read. Since the Bible is such an important book—in fact, *the* most important book—readers want to be sure that they are using an accurate and understandable translation of the original text. It would be wonderful if everyone could read the Bible in the original languages: Hebrew, Aramaic, and Greek. Since so very few have learned these ancient languages, nearly everyone depends on translations.

This book serves as a guide to the English Bible and English Bible translations. This guide should help you understand how we got the Bible, what are the important ancient manuscripts, and what are the significant English translations that have been made throughout history. This book should also guide you in your selection of Bible versions and give you direction in using each one.

The first chapter focuses on how the Bible, God's inspired Word, was first written. Chapters 2 and 3 explain how the Old Testament and New Testament were written and compiled and what ancient manuscripts still exist. The next three chapters provide a history of the English Bible—from the earliest versions in the seventh century to the King James Version, from the King James Version to the Revised Standard Version, and the modern translations of the last forty years. The seventh chapter looks at different ways of translating, and the last chapter provides a close comparative study of several modern translations of the prologue to John's Gospel.

THE INSPIRATION OF SCRIPTURE
How the Bible Was First Written and by Whom

When was the last time you took the big black book down from the shelf and opened it? You have to admit, there's something wonderful about the title: the *Holy Bible*. Some have called it the Good Book. True. But there's a better title: the *God* Book—for it is God's written communication to the world. The Bible contains everything that God wants to tell us—everything about himself, his creation, and us.

Of all the millions of books there are in the world, there is only one that was authored by God. And there is only one book that reveals God's plan for man. It is an amazing book because it has a divine author and because it tells the wonderful story of God's love for us. But there is another amazing story—the story of how the Bible came to us.

The Bible was originally written in ancient languages (Hebrew, Aramaic, and Greek) by men who were inspired by God. The Bible itself tells us that it is an inspired text. It says, "All Scripture is God-inspired." [1] A translation closer to the original language (Greek) would be, "All scripture is God-breathed." This tells us that every word of the Bible was breathed out from God. The words of the Bible came from God and were written by men. The apostle Peter affirmed this when he said that "no prophecy of Scripture came about by the prophet's own interpretation. For prophecy never had its origin in the will of man, but men spoke from God as they were carried along by the Holy Spirit." [2]

"Men spoke from God." This short sentence is the key to understanding how the Bible came into being. Thousands of years ago, God chose certain men—such as Moses, David, Isaiah, Jeremiah, Ezekiel, and Daniel—to receive his words and write them down. What they wrote became books, or sections, of the Old Testament. Nearly two thousand years ago, God chose other men—such as Matthew, Mark, Luke, John, and Paul—to communicate his new message, the message of salvation through Jesus Christ. What they wrote became books, or sections, of the New Testament.

God gave his words to these men in many different ways. Certain writers of the Old Testament received messages directly from God. Moses was given the Ten Commandments inscribed on a stone when he was in God's presence on Mount Sinai. When David was composing his psalms to God, he received divine inspiration to foretell certain events that would occur a thousand years later in Jesus Christ's life. God told his prophets—such as Isaiah and Jeremiah—exactly what to say; therefore, when they gave a message, it was God's word, not their own. This is why many Old Testament prophets often said, "Thus says the Lord." (This statement appears over two thousand times in the Old Testament). To other prophets, such as Ezekiel and Daniel, God communicated his message through visions and dreams. They recorded exactly what they saw, whether they understood it or not. And other Old Testament writers, such as Samuel and Ezra, were directed by God to record events in the history of Israel.

Four hundred years after the last book of the Old Testament (Malachi) was written, God's Son, Jesus Christ, came to earth. In his talks, he affirmed the divine authorship of the Old Testament writings.[3] Furthermore, he often pointed to certain passages in the Old Testament as having predicted certain events in his life.[4] The New Testament writers also affirmed the divine inspiration of the Old Testament text. It was the apostle Paul who was directed by God to write, "all Scripture is God-inspired." Quite specifically, he was speaking of the Old Testament. And, as was already noted, Peter said that the Old Testament prophets were motivated by the Holy Spirit to speak from God.

The New Testament is also a God-inspired book. Before Jesus left this earth and returned to his

Father, he told the disciples that he would send the Holy Spirit to them. He told them that one of the functions of the Holy Spirit would be to remind them of all the things that Jesus had said and then to guide them into more truth.[5] Those who wrote the Gospels were helped by the Holy Spirit to remember Jesus' exact words, and those who wrote other parts of the New Testament were guided by the Spirit as they wrote.

The apostle Paul indicated that the New Testament apostles were taught by the Holy Spirit what to say. The writers of the New Testament did not speak with words "taught by human wisdom," but with "words taught by the Holy Spirit." [6] What they wrote was Spirit taught. For example, when the apostle John saw that Jesus Christ had come to give eternal life to men, the Spirit helped him express this truth in many different ways. Thus, the reader of John's Gospel sees different phrases about Jesus giving life: "in him was life," "a well of living water springing up into eternal life," "the bread of life," "the light of life," "the resurrection and the life," etc.[7] When the apostle Paul contemplated the fullness of Christ's deity, he was inspired by the Spirit to use such phrasing as "in him dwells all the fullness of the Godhead bodily," "in him are hid all the treasures of wisdom and knowledge," and "the unsearchable riches of Christ." [8]

6

As the Spirit taught the writers, they used their own vocabulary and writing style to express the thought of the Spirit. As such, the Scriptures came as the result of divine and human cooperation. The Scriptures were not mechanically inspired—as if God used the men as machines through whom he dictated the divine utterance. Rather, the Scriptures were inspired by God, then written by men. The Bible, therefore, is both fully divine and fully human.

The next time you open that big black book called the *Holy Bible,* remember that you are reading the book produced by one divine authority with many human authors. God originated his Word and now sustains it with his presence. It is an inspired and inspiring Book.

NOTES

[1]See 2 Timothy 3:16, KJV.
[2]See 2 Peter 1:20-21, NIV.
[3]See Matthew 5:17-19; Luke 16:17; John 10:35.
[4]See Luke 24:27, 44.
[5]See John 14:26; 15:26; 16:13-15.
[6]See 1 Corinthians 2:10-13.
[7]See John 1:4; 4:14; 6:48; 8:12; 11:25; 14:6.
[8]See Colossians 2:9; 2:3; Ephesians 3:8.

THE OLD TESTAMENT TEXT
*How It Was Made
and the Manuscripts
We Have Today*

THE OLD TESTAMENT

The Bible is composed of two main sections: the Old Testament and the New Testament. The word *testament* means "covenant" or "agreement." [1] The old covenant was based primarily on the agreement between God and his people concerning the law. God promised to bless his people if they kept his commandments. His people often failed to keep his commandments; therefore, the old covenant was flawed. However, this did not stop God. He told his people through some of his prophets that he would enact a new covenant—one in which he would write his laws, not on stone tablets (as he had done with the Ten Commandments), but on the very hearts of men and women. [2] The new covenant became a reality when God's Son, Jesus Christ, came to earth. He enacted a new covenant that was based on having faith in him. Everyone participating in the new covenant believes that Jesus is the Son of God, who died on the cross to redeem mankind and rose from the dead to enliven them. The Old Testament focuses on the old covenant between God and his people. The New Testament focuses on God's new covenant with every believer.

During the time of the old covenant, God inspired several godly men to give his Word to his people, the Israelites. These writings were kept and collected into three major sections: the Law, the Prophets, and the Writings. When Jesus spoke to his disciples about the Old Testament, he referred to this same threefold division when he said, "This is what I told you while I was still with you: Everything must be fulfilled that is written about me in the Law of Moses, the Prophets and the Psalms [which are part of "the Writings"]." [3]

Of the three sections, the most important to the Israelites has always been the Law. Another name for the Law is the Pentateuch (literally, "five in a case"—referring to five scrolls in a case); the Pentateuch contains the first five books of the Bible: Genesis, Exodus, Leviticus, Numbers, and Deuteronomy. The Pentateuch, said to be written by Moses, has provided the Israelites with basic teachings and principles for personal, social, and spiritual life. In short, it contains the essence of Judaism.

"The Prophets" comprise a very large segment of the Hebrew Bible. "The Prophets" include four historical books (Joshua, Judges, Samuel, and Kings), the books of the three great prophets

(Isaiah, Jeremiah, and Ezekiel), and the books of
the twelve minor prophets (Hosea, Joel, Amos,
Obadiah, Jonah, Micah, Nahum, Habbakuk,
Zephaniah, Haggai, Zechariah, and Malachi). The
prophetic books are a record of God's oracles to
his people concerning past, present, and future
events.

In the Hebrew Bible, "the Writings," comprising
the last section, are of two kinds. The first is called
"Wisdom Writings"; this includes Psalms, Proverbs,
Job, the Song of Solomon, Lamentations, and
Ecclesiastes. Most of these books are poetic in
form and thought, and many of them, especially
Job, Proverbs, and Ecclesiastes, purport "wisdom"
as a central theme. The second kind of "Wisdom
Writings" includes historical books, specifically
Esther, Daniel, Ezra, Nehemiah, and Chronicles.

The grouping and ordering of the books in
the Hebrew Bible is different from what Christians
have in their Bibles because the Christian Bible
adopted the order in the Septuagint, a Greek
translation of the Hebrew Bible. The Septuagint,
the first translation of the Hebrew Bible, was made
in the third century B.C. by Jewish scribes versed
in Hebrew and Greek. This translation became
very popular among Jews in the first two centuries
before Christ because many Jews in those days did
not understand Hebrew. Their ancestors had left

Israel centuries before, and generation after generation gradually lost the ability to read the Scriptures in Hebrew. Many of the Jews in Jesus' day used the Septuagint as their Bible. Quite naturally, the early Christians also used the Septuagint in their meetings and for personal reading; and many of the New Testament apostles quoted it when they wrote the Gospels and Epistles in Greek.

The order of the books in the Septuagint is the same order in our Bibles today. For the sake of memorization, it is convenient to divide the Old Testament into five sections:

1. THE PENTATEUCH (THE LAW)
   Genesis
   Exodus
   Leviticus
   Numbers
   Deuteronomy

2. HISTORICAL WRITINGS
   Joshua
   Judges
   Ruth
   1 and 2 Samuel
   1 and 2 Kings
   1 and 2 Chronicles

Ezra
Nehemiah
Esther

3. WISDOM LITERATURE (OR POETRY)
   Job
   Psalms
   Proverbs
   Ecclesiastes
   Song of Songs

4. MAJOR PROPHETS
   Isaiah
   Jeremiah
   Lamentations
   Ezekiel
   Daniel

5. MINOR PROPHETS
   Hosea
   Joel
   Amos
   Obadiah
   Jonah
   Micah
   Nahum
   Habbakuk
   Zephaniah

Haggai
Zechariah
Malachi

OLD TESTAMENT MANUSCRIPTS

Not one of the original writings (called "the auto-graphs") of any book in the Old Testament still exists today. Fortunately, Jewish scribes throughout the ages have made copies of God's Word. Jewish scribes took meticulous care in producing copies of the Scripture because they regarded the text as being God given and God inspired as to the very letter. Jesus had the same regard for the Old Testament text; on several occasions he affirmed the immutability of the text—even down to the very letter.[4]

In ancient times scribes used quill, ink, and leather scrolls to make copies of individual books of the Bible. Some of the scrolls, made of several treated animal hides stitched together, could be as long as thirty-five to forty feet when unrolled. As scrolls wore out or if there was a need for copies in various synagogues, Jewish scribes would make additional copies—and they did so with painstaking care. It is known that scribes would count the number of letters on the new copy and compare it with the exemplar in an attempt to find even one letter difference between the two. If the copy was in error, it would be corrected or destroyed. This practice continued generation after generation and century after century. Beginning in the sixth century and into the tenth century A.D., certain European Jewish scribes called the Masoretes worked carefully to preserve the Old Testament text as they transmitted it from copy to copy. The Hebrew word *masora* means "that which is transmitted," "that which is handed down"; hence, the name—Masoretes. Several of the manuscripts they produced still exist. Some of the more important Masoretic manuscripts are as follows:

The Cairo Codex of the Prophets (A.D. 895), containing the Prophets

The British Museum Codex Oriental 4445 (Ninth or tenth century), containing a large portion of the Pentateuch

The Leningrad Codex of the Prophets (A.D. 916), containing the Major Prophets

The Leningrad Codex (A.D. 1008–09), having the complete Old Testament text

The Aleppo Codex (A.D. 900–925), originally containing the entire Old Testament text but now with a quarter of its text missing.[5]

Until the middle of the twentieth century, the Masoretic manuscripts were the oldest ones in existence. Then in 1947 and 1948, the year Israel regained its national independence, there was a phenomenal discovery. A bedouin shepherd boy found scrolls in a cave west of the Dead Sea. These scrolls, known as the Dead Sea Scrolls, are dated between 100 B.C. and A.D. 100. They are nearly a thousand years earlier than any of the Masoretic manuscripts. The Dead Sea Scrolls contain significant portions of the Old Testament. Every book except Esther is represented. The largest portions come from the Pentateuch (especially Deuteronomy—twenty-five manuscripts), the major Prophets (especially Isaiah—eighteen manuscripts), and Psalms (twenty-seven manuscripts). The Dead Sea Scrolls also have portions of the Septuagint, the Targums (an Aramaic translation of the Old Testament), some apocryphal fragments, and a commentary on Habakkuk. The scribes who made these scrolls were members of a community of ascetic Jews who lived in Qumran from the third century B.C. to the first century A.D.

Even though the Dead Sea Scrolls are nearly a thousand years older than the Masoretic manuscripts, there are not as many significant differences between the two groups of manuscripts as one would expect. Normally, a thousand years of copying would have generated thousands of differences in wording. But this is not the case when one compares most of the Dead Sea Scrolls with the Masoretic manuscripts. This shows that Jewish scribes for over a millennium copied one form of the text with extreme fidelity.

To this day, almost all Bible scholars still use the Masoretic Text of the Hebrew Bible as the authoritative, standard text. At the same time, they make use of the findings of the Dead Sea Scrolls, as well as two other important sources: the Septuagint and the Samaritan Pentateuch (i.e., the Pentateuch as transcribed and edited by the Samaritans).[6] The Masoretic Text with up-to-date textual notes is published in an edition called *Biblia Hebraica Stuttgartensia*.

NOTES

[1]The word *testament* goes back through Latin *testamentum* to Greek, *diatheke*.

[2]See Jeremiah 31:31-34.

[3]See Luke 24:44.

[4]See Matthew 5:17-18; John 10:35.

[5]See "Biblical Manuscripts" by Philip W. Comfort in *Young's Compact Bible Dictionary* (Wheaton, Ill.: Tyndale House Publishers, 1989), from which this portion was adapted.

[6]Some of the manuscripts discovered in Qumran, especially two manuscripts of 1 Samuel, show greater affinity with the Septuagint than with Masoretic Text; and other manuscripts from Qumran, especially one manuscript of Exodus, resemble the Samaritan

Pentateuch. Thus, there must have been some different forms of the text other than the one appearing in most of the Dead Sea Scrolls and then later in the Masoretic manuscripts. However, scholars still rely, for the most part, on the Masoretic Text and use the other sources as supplements.

THE NEW TESTAMENT TEXT
*How It Was Made
and the Manuscripts
We Have Today*

THE NEW TESTAMENT

Whereas the Old Testament took hundreds of years to be written, the New Testament was completed within the span of fifty years, during the second half of the first century A.D. Most likely, the earliest Gospel was written by Mark (c. 50–55). According to tradition, John Mark used Peter's sermons to compose a narrative Gospel. This simple and straightforward account portrays Jesus as the Son of God and servant of God. Apparently, both Matthew and Luke used Mark's Gospel when they wrote their own. The Gospel of Matthew was written around A.D. 70; it focuses on the message of the messianic King and his kingdom. Luke wrote his Gospel (c. 60) as the result of investigating Jesus' life and ministry from their beginnings. Luke wrote a sequel, the book of Acts, which is a detailed account of how the early church grew and spread after Jesus' resurrection and ascension, followed by the outpouring of the Holy Spirit. John's Gospel was written late in the first century (c. 85–90). He wrote his Gospel to encourage faith in Jesus Christ as God's Son, the giver of eternal life.

After the four Gospels and Acts, according to the arrangement in our Bibles, are Paul's epistles, of which there are thirteen. They are: Romans (c. 58), 1 and 2 Corinthians (c. 56–57), Galatians (49 or 56), Ephesians (61), Philippians (62), Colossians (62), 1 and 2 Thessalonians (c. 51), 1 and 2 Timothy (c. 63, 66), Titus (c. 65), and Philemon (c. 61). These epistles can be placed in three categories: (1) epistles to specific churches prior to Paul's imprisonment (Romans, 1 and 2 Corinthians, Galatians, 1 and 2 Thessalonians), (2) epistles written during Paul's imprisonment in Rome—otherwise known as the Prison Epistles (Ephesians, Philippians, Colossians, and Philemon), and (3) epistles written to individuals giving advice concerning the care of particular local churches—otherwise known as the Pastoral Epistles (1 and 2 Timothy, Titus). Although a few scholars think Paul wrote Hebrews, it is unlikely. The author of that epistle wrote in a style very different from Paul's, and the author was addressing Jewish Christians only, while Paul's ministry was committed primarily to Gentile Christians. To this day, no one knows who wrote Hebrews; it may have been Apollos or Barnabas or Priscilla—or even some other Jewish Christian who was one of Paul's co-workers.

Following Paul's epistles are the General Epistles and Revelation. James, the elder of Jerusalem and brother of Jesus, wrote an epistle to Jewish Christians who had fled from Jerusalem due to persecution.[1] His letter, dated around 45, is the earliest piece of writing to be included in the New Testament. Peter wrote two letters—one to encourage Christians undergoing trials and the other to warn Christians against false prophets (c. 63, 66). John wrote three epistles—one that corresponds perfectly to the style and emphasis of his Gospel and two to individuals (c. 85–90). Jude, the brother of James and Jesus, wrote a brief letter warning believers against false prophets (c. 75). And John penned the last book, Revelation (c. 90–95).

After the various books of the New Testament were written and began to circulate among the churches, Christians collected certain books into single volumes. In the first century, each of the four Gospels was treated as an individual book about Jesus' life and ministry. Beginning in the late second century, Christians began to collect the four Gospels into one volume. This collection became known as "The Gospel: According to Matthew, According to Mark, According to Luke, According to John." Paul's epistles were also collected into a single volume—perhaps as early as 85–90. Later, in the second and third centuries, other Christians began to combine Acts with the General Epistles in one volume.

In the first century, Christians treated the Old Testament as their "Scriptures." They read the Old Testament and spoke from it in their meetings.[2] They also had the living word of the apostles who were present among them. The apostles taught them the gospel and passed on to them the teachings of Jesus. But after the apostles died, Christians depended more and more on what the apostles had written. At the same time, they began to recognize that their writings were on the same par as the Old Testament writings. In short, several of the books of the New Testament were considered as early as the second century to be divinely inspired Scripture: the four Gospels, Acts, Paul's epistles, 1 Peter, and 1 John. Other books took longer to gain full recognition: Hebrews (because the author was unknown), James (because it was thought to have doctrinal differences with Paul's theology on salvation), 2 Peter and Jude (over the question of authorship), 2 and 3 John (because they were not well known), and Revelation (because its message and authorship were debated). Once the issues were resolved, in the middle of the fourth century, these books were also accepted by the church as being divinely inspired and worthy of inclusion in the New Testament canon.[3]

NEW TESTAMENT MANUSCRIPTS

Christians began to make copies of the New Testament writings before the end of the first century. The early Christians were among the first to use the form of a book called a codex, instead of a scroll. A codex was constructed much like our modern books by folding sheets of papyrus or vellum (treated animal hide) in the middle and then sewing them together at the spine. This kind of book was advantageous because (1) it enabled the scribe to write on both sides; (2) it facilitated easier access to particular passages (as opposed to a scroll, which had to be unrolled); (3) it enabled Christians to bind together all four Gospels or all Paul's epistles or any other such combination; and (4) it made it easier for any individual or local church to make its own volume of the New Testament or any portion thereof.

Because not one original writing (autograph) of any New Testament book still exists, we depend on copies for reconstructing the original text. According to most scholars, the closest copy to an autograph is a papyrus manuscript designated P52, dated around 110–125, containing a few verses of John 18 (31-34, 37-38). This fragment, only twenty to thirty years removed from the autograph, was part of one of the earliest copies of John's Gospel. A few scholars, however, believe that there is an even earlier manuscript, designated P46. This manuscript, known as the Chester Beatty Papyrus II, containing all of Paul's epistles except the Pastorals, has recently been dated in the late first century.[4] If this dating is accurate, then we have an entire collecion of Paul's epistles that must have been made only twenty to thirty years after Paul wrote most of the Epistles. We possess many other early copies of various parts of the New Testament; several of the papyrus manuscripts are dated from the late second century to the early fourth century. Some of the most important New Testament papyrus manuscripts are as follows:

THE OXYRHYNCHUS PAPYRI

Beginning in 1898 Grenfell and Hunt discovered thousands of papyrus fragments in the ancient rubbish heaps of Oxyrhynchus, Egypt. This site yielded volumes of papyrus fragments containing all sorts of written material (literature, business and legal contracts, letters, etc.) as well as over thirty-five manuscripts containing portions of the New Testament. Some of the more noteworthy papyrus manuscripts are P1 (Matthew 1), P5 (John 1, 16), P13 (Hebrews 2–5, 10–12), and P22 (John 15–16).

BR $3.95

COMPLETE GUIDE TO BIBLE VERSIO
COMFORT P   TYM 07 1251-X
M-MKT   ABK

084-231-251X   QTY_____

LOGOS OF WESTWOOD
0000113   ***
          9- 9-91   AAA

THE CHESTER BEATTY PAPYRI (NAMED AFTER THE OWNER, CHESTER BEATTY)

These manuscripts were purchased from a dealer in Egypt during the 1930s by Chester Beatty and by the University of Michigan. The three manuscripts in this collection are very early and contain a large portion of the New Testament text. P45 (third century) contains portions of all four Gospels and Acts; P46 (late first century) has almost all of Paul's epistles and Hebrews; and P47 (third century) contains Revelation 9–17.

THE BODMER PAPYRI (NAMED AFTER THE OWNER, M. MARTIN BODMER)

These manuscripts were purchased from a dealer in Egypt during the 1950s and 1960s. The three important papyri in this collection are P66 (c. 175, containing almost all of John), P72 (third century, having all of 1 and 2 Peter and Jude), and P75 (c. 200, containing large parts of Luke 3—John 15).[5]

During the twentieth century, nearly a hundred papyrus manuscripts containing portions of the New Testament were discovered. In previous centuries, especially the nineteenth, other manuscripts were discovered—several of which date in the fourth or fifth century. The most noteworthy manuscripts are as follows:

CODEX SINAITICUS

This manuscript was discovered by Constantin von Tischendorf in St. Catherine's Monastery situated at the foot of Mount Sinai. It dates around A.D. 350, contains the entire New Testament, and provides an early and fairly reliable witness to the New Testament autographs.

CODEX VATICANUS

This manuscript had been in the Vatican's library since at least 1481, but it was not made available to scholars, like Tischendorf and Tregelles, until the middle of the nineteenth century. This codex, dated slightly earlier than Sinaiticus, has both the Old Testament and New Testament in Greek, excluding the last part of the New Testament (from Hebrews 9:15 to the end of Revelation) and the Pastoral Epistles. For the most part, scholars have commended Codex Vaticanus for being one of the most trustworthy witnesses to the New Testament text.

CODEX ALEXANDRINUS

This is a fifth century manuscript, displaying nearly all of the New Testament. It is known to be a very reliable witness to the General Epistles and Revelation.

CODEX EPHRAEMI RESCRIPTUS

This is a fifth century document containing a large portion of the New Testament—partially erased and written upon with the sermons of St. Ephraem—later deciphered by the painstaking efforts of Tischendorf.

CODEX BEZAE

This is a fifth century manuscript named after Theodore Beza, its discoverer, containing the Gospels and Acts and displaying a text quite different from the manuscripts mentioned above.

CODEX WASHINGTONIANUS (OR, *THE FREER GOSPELS*—NAMED AFTER ITS OWNER, CHARLES FREER)

This is a fifth century manuscript containing all four Gospels housed in the Smithsonian Institution in Washington, D.C.[6]

Prior to the fifteenth century when Johannes Gutenberg invented movable type for the printing press, all copies of any work of literature were made by hand (hence, the name *manuscript*). At present, we have more than 6,000 manuscript copies of the Greek New Testament or portions thereof. No other work of Greek literature can boast of such numbers. Homer's *Iliad,* the greatest of all Greek classical works, is extant in about 650 manuscripts; and Euripides' tragedies exist in about 330 manuscripts. The numbers on all the other works of Greek literature are far less. Furthermore, it must be said that the amount of time between the original composition and the next surviving manuscript is far less for the New Testament than for any other work in Greek literature. The lapse for most classical Greek works is about eight hundred to a thousand years; whereas the lapse for many books in the New Testament is around one hundred years. Because of the abundant wealth of manuscripts and because several of the manuscripts are dated in the early centuries of the church, New Testament textual scholars have a great advantage over classical textual scholars. The New Testament scholars have the resources to reconstruct the original text of the New Testament with great accuracy, and they have produced some excellent editions of the Greek New Testament.[7]

Finally, it must be said that, although there are certainly differences in many of the New Testament manuscripts, not one fundamental doctrine of the Christian faith rests on a disputed reading. Frederic Kenyon, a renowned paleographer and textual critic, affirmed this when he said, "The Christian can take the whole Bible in his hand and say without fear or hesitation that he holds in it the true Word of God, handed down without essential loss from generation to generation throughout the centuries."[8]

NOTES

[1]See Acts 8:1.

[2]See 1 Corinthians 14:26; Ephesians 5:19; Colossians 3:16; 2 Timothy 3:14-17.

[3]The word *canon* comes from the Greek word *kanon,* meaning "rule" or "measure." A canon, therefore, indicates a standard of measurement. Before a book could be included in the New Testament canon, it had to measure up to this standard: (1) it had to be authored by an apostle, an associate of an apostle, or a relative of Jesus (i.e., James and Jude); and (2) it had to contain divinely inspired truths that could be taught as Christian doctrine.

[4]See Young-Kyu Kim's article, "The Paleographic Dating of P46 to the Later First Century," in *Biblica,* 1988, 248–57.

[5]For a more complete list of the early papyrus manuscripts and a thorough discussion concerning their effect on the Greek New Testament text, see *Early Manuscripts and Modern Translations of the New Testament* (Wheaton, Ill.: Tyndale House Publishers, 1990) by Philip W. Comfort.

[6]See "Biblical Manuscripts," by Philip W. Comfort in *Young's Compact Bible Dictionary,* (Wheaton, Ill.: Tyndale House Publishers, 1989) from which this portion was adapted.

[7]The two best editions of the Greek New Testament are the *Greek New Testament,* published by the United Bible Societies (3d corrected ed., 1983) and *Novum Testamentum Graece,* edited by Eberhard and Erwin Nestle, followed by Kurt Aland (26th ed., 1979). These two volumes, which have the same text but differ as to punctuation and textual notes, represent the best in modern textual scholarship.

[8]Frederic Kenyon, *Our Bible and the Ancient Manuscripts* (New York: Harper and Row, 1958), 55.

THE STORY OF THE ENGLISH BIBLE
From the First English Versions to the King James Version

As the gospel spread and churches
multiplied in the early centuries of the Christian era,
Christians in various countries wanted to read the
Bible in their own language. As a result, many translations were made in several different languages—
as early as the second century. For example, there
were translations done in Coptic for the Egyptians,
in Syriac for those whose language was Aramaic, in
Gothic for the Germanic people called the Goths,
and in Latin for the Romans and Carthagenians. The
most famous Latin translation was done by Jerome
around 400. This translation, known as the Latin
Vulgate (*vulgate* meaning "common"—hence, the
Latin text for the common man), was used exten-
sively in the Roman Catholic church for centuries
and centuries.

EARLY TRANSLATIONS: CAEDMON'S, BEDE'S, ALFRED THE GREAT'S

The gospel was brought to England by missionaries
from Rome in the sixth century. The Bible they carried with them was the Latin Vulgate. The Christians
living in England at that time depended on monks

for any kind of instruction from the Bible. The monks read and taught the Latin Bible. After a few centuries, when more monasteries were founded, the need arose for translations of the Bible in English. The earliest English translation, as far as we know, is one done by a seventh century monk named Caedmon, who made a metrical version of parts of the Old and New Testaments. Another English churchman, named Bede, is said to have translated the Gospels into English. Tradition has it that he was translating the Gospel of John on his deathbed in 735. Another translator was Alfred the Great (reigned 871–899), who was regarded as a very literate king. He included in his laws parts of the Ten Commandments translated into English, and he also translated the Psalms.

OTHER EARLY VERSIONS: LINDISFARNE GOSPELS, SHOREHAM'S PSALMS, ROLLE'S PSALMS

All translations of the English Bible prior to the work of Tyndale (discussed later) were done from the Latin text. Some Latin versions of the Gospels with word-for-word English translations written between the lines, which are called interlinear translations, survive from the tenth century. The most famous translation of this period is called the *Lindisfarne Gospels* (950).[1] In the late tenth century, Aelfric (c. 955–1020), abbot of Eynsham, made idiomatic translations of various parts of the Bible. Two of these translations still exist. Later, in the 1300s, William of Shoreham translated the Psalms into English and so did Richard Rolle, whose editions of the Psalms included a verse-by-verse commentary. Both of these translations, which were metrical and therefore called Psalters, were popular when John Wycliffe was a young man.

WYCLIFFE'S VERSION

John Wycliffe (c. 1329–1384), the most eminent Oxford theologian of his day, and his associates, were the first to translated the entire Bible from Latin into English. Wycliffe has been called the "morningstar of the Reformation" because he boldly questioned papal authority, criticized the sale of indulgences (which were supposed to release a person from punishment in purgatory), denied the reality of transubstantiation (the doctrine that the bread and wine are changed into Jesus Christ's body and blood during Communion), and spoke out against church hierarchies. The pope reproved Wycliffe for his heretical teachings and asked that Oxford University dismiss him. But Oxford and many government leaders stood with Wycliffe, so he was able to survive the pope's assaults.

Wycliffe believed that the way to prevail in his struggle with the church's abusive authority was to make the Bible available to the people in their own language. Then, they could read for themselves about how each one of them could have a personal relationship with God through Christ Jesus—apart from any ecclesiastical authority. Wycliffe, with his associates, completed the New Testament around 1380 and the Old Testament in 1382.[2] Wycliffe concentrated his labors on the New Testament, while an associate, Nicholas of Hereford, did a major part of the Old Testament. Wycliffe and his co-workers, unfamiliar with the original Hebrew and Greek, translated the Latin text into English.

After Wycliffe finished the translation work, he organized a group of poor parishioners, known as Lollards, to go throughout England preaching Christian truths and reading the Scriptures in their mother tongue to all who would hear God's Word. As a result the Word of God, through Wycliffe's translation, became available to many Englishmen. He was loved and yet hated. His ecclesiastical enemies did not forget his opposition to their power or his successful efforts in making the Scriptures available to all. Several decades after he died, they condemned him for heresy, dug up his body, burned it, and threw his ashes into the Swift River.

One of Wycliffe's close associates, John Purvey (c. 1353–1428), continued Wycliffe's work by producing a revision of his translation in 1388. Purvey was an excellent scholar; his work was very well received by his generation and following generations. Within less than a century, Purvey's revision had replaced the original Wycliffe Bible.[3]

As was stated before, Wycliffe and his associates were the first Englishmen to translate the entire Bible into English from Latin. Therefore, their Bible was a translation of a translation, not a translation of the original languages. With the coming of the Renaissance came the resurgence of the study of the classics—and with it the resurgence of the study of Greek, as well as Hebrew. Thus, for the first time in nearly a thousand years (500–1500—the approximate time when Latin was the dominant language for scholarship, except in the Greek church) scholars began to read the New Testament in its original language, Greek. By 1500, Greek was being taught at Oxford.

TYNDALE'S TRANSLATION

William Tyndale was born in the age of the Renaissance. He graduated in 1515 from Oxford, where he had studied the Scriptures in Greek and in Hebrew. By the time he was thirty, Tyndale had committed his life to translating the Bible from the original languages into English. His heart's desire is exemplified in a statement he made to a clergyman when refuting the view that only the clergy were qualified to read and correctly interpret the Scriptures. Tyndale said, "If God spare my life, ere many years, I will cause a boy that driveth the plough to know more of the Scripture than thou dost."[4]

In 1523 Tyndale went to London seeking a place to work on his translation. When the bishop of London would not give him hospitality, he was provided a place by Humphrey Munmouth, a cloth merchant. Then, in 1524, Tyndale left England for Germany because the English church, which was still under the papal authority of Rome, strongly opposed putting the Bible into the hands of the laity. Tyndale first settled in Hamburg, Germany. Quite possibly, he met Luther in Wittenberg soon thereafter. Even if he didn't meet Luther, he was well acquainted with Luther's writings and Luther's German translation of the New Testament (published in 1522). Both Luther and Tyndale used the same Greek text (one compiled by Erasmus in 1516) in making their translations.

Tyndale completed his translation of the New Testament in 1525. Fifteen thousand copies, in six editions, were smuggled into England between the years 1525 and 1530. Church authorities did

their best to confiscate copies of Tyndale's translation and burn them, but they couldn't stop the
flow of Bibles from Germany into England. Tyndale
himself could not return to England because
he had been condemned at the same time his
translation had been banned. However, he continued to work abroad—correcting, revising, and
reissuing his translation until his final revision
appeared in 1535. Shortly thereafter, in May of
1535, Tyndale was arrested and carried off to
a castle near Brussels. After being in prison for
over a year, he was tried and condemned to death.
He was strangled and burnt at the stake on October
6, 1536. His final words were so very poignant:
"Lord, open the King of England's eyes."[5]

After finishing the New Testament, Tyndale
had begun work on a translation of the Hebrew
Old Testament, but he did not live long enough
to complete his task. He had, however, translated
the Pentateuch (the first five books of the Old
Testament), Jonah, and some historical books.
While Tyndale was in prison, an associate of his
named Miles Coverdale (1488–1569) brought to
completion an entire Bible in English—based
largely on Tyndale's translation of the New Testament and other Old Testament books. In other
words, Coverdale finished what Tyndale had
begun.

COVERDALE'S VERSION

Miles Coverdale was a Cambridge graduate who, like Tyndale, was forced to flee England because he had been strongly influenced by Luther to the extent that he was boldly preaching against Roman Catholic doctrine. While he was abroad, Coverdale met Tyndale and then served as an assistant—especially helping Tyndale translate the Pentateuch. By the time Coverdale produced a complete translation (1537), the king of England, Henry VIII, had broken all ties with the pope and was ready to see the appearance of an English Bible.[6] Perhaps Tyndale's prayer had been answered—with a very ironic twist. The King gave his royal approval to Coverdale's translation without knowing that he was endorsing the work of the man he had earlier condemned.

THOMAS MATTHEW'S VERSION AND THE GREAT BIBLE

In the same year that Coverdale's Bible was endorsed by the king (1537), another Bible was published in England. This was the work of one called Thomas Matthew, a pseudonym for John Rogers (c. 1500–1555), a friend of Tyndale. Evidently, Rogers used Tyndale's unpublished translation of the Old Testament

historical books, other parts of Tyndale's translation, and still other parts of Coverdale's translation,
to form an entire Bible. This Bible also received
the king's approval. Matthew's Bible was revised
in 1538 and printed for distribution in the churches
throughout England. This Bible, called the Great
Bible because of its size and costliness, became
the first English Bible authorized for public use.

Many editions of the Great Bible were printed
in the early 1540s. However, its distribution
was limited. Furthermore, King Henry's attitude
about the new translation changed. As a result,
the English Parliament passed a law in 1543 for-
bidding the use of any English translation. It was
a crime for any unlicensed person to read or
explain the Scriptures in public. Many copies of
Tyndale's New Testament and Coverdale's Bible
were burned in London.

Greater repression was to follow. After a short
period of leniency (during the reign of Edward VI,
1547–1553), severe persecution came from the
hands of Mary. She was a Roman Catholic who
was determined to restore Catholicism to England
and repress Protestantism. Many Protestants were
executed, including John Rogers and Thomas
Cranmer, the Bible translators. Coverdale was
arrested, then released. He fled to Geneva, a sanctu-
ary for English Protestants.

THE GENEVA BIBLE AND
THE BISHOPS' BIBLE

The English exiles in Geneva chose William
Whittingham (c. 1524–1579) to make an English
translation of the New Testament for them. He used
Theodore Beza's Latin translation and consulted the
Greek text. This Bible became very popular because
it was small and moderately priced. The preface to
the Bible and its many annotations were affected by
a strong evangelical influence, as well as by the
teachings of John Calvin. Calvin was one of the greatest thinkers of the Reformation, a renowned biblical
commentator, and the principle leader in Geneva
during those days.

While the Geneva Bible was popular among
many English men and women, it was not accept-
able among many leaders in the Church of England
because of its Calvinistic notes. These leaders, rec-
ognizing that the Great Bible was inferior to the
Geneva Bible in style and scholarship, initiated a
revision of the Great Bible. This revised Bible, published in 1568, became known as the Bishops'
Bible; it continued in use until it was superseded by
the King James Version of 1611.

THE KING JAMES VERSION

After James VI of Scotland became the king of
England (known as James I), he invited several

clergymen from Puritan and Anglican factions to meet together with the hope that differences could be reconciled. The meeting did not achieve this. However, during the meeting one of the Puritan leaders, John Reynolds, president of Corpus Christi College, Oxford, asked the king to authorize a new translation because he wanted to see a translation that was more accurate than previous translations. King James liked this idea because the Bishops' Bible had not been successful and because he considered the notes in the Geneva Bible to be seditious. The king initiated the work and took an active part in planning the new translation. He suggested that university professors work on the translation to assure the best scholarship, and he strongly urged that they should not have any marginal notes besides those pertaining to literal renderings from the Hebrew and Greek. The absence of interpretive notes would help the translation be accepted by all the churches in England.

More than fifty scholars, trained in Hebrew and Greek, began the work in 1607. The translation went through several committees before it was finalized. The scholars were instructed to follow the Bishops' Bible as the basic version, as long as it adhered to the original text, and to consult the translations of Tyndale, Matthew, and Coverdale, as well as the Great Bible and the Geneva Bible when they appeared to contain more accurate renderings of the original languages. This dependence on other versions is expressed in the preface to the King James Version: "Truly, good Christian reader, we never thought from the beginning that we should need to make a new translation, nor yet to make of a bad one a good one . . . but to make a good one better, or out of many good ones one principal good one."

The King James Version captured the best of all the preceding English translations and far exceeded all of them. This is aptly expressed by J. H. Skilton:

> The Authorized Version gathered to itself the virtues of the long and brilliant line of English Bible translations; it united high scholarship with Christian devotion and piety. It came into being at a time when the English language was vigorous and young, and its scholars had a remarkable mastery of the instrument [talent] which Providence had prepared for them. Their version has justifiably been called "the noblest monument of English prose.[7]

Indeed, the King James Version, known in England as the Authorized Version because it was authorized by the king, has become an enduring monument of English prose because of its gracious style, majestic language, and poetic rhythms. No other book has had such a tremendous influence on English literature, and no other translation has touched the lives of so many English-speaking people for centuries and centuries, even until the present day.

NOTES

[1] *The Lindisfarne Gospels,* also known as the *Book of Durham* or *The Gospels of St. Cuthbert.*

[2] The original manuscript has been kept at the Bodleian Library in Oxford.

[3] There are about 170 extant manuscripts of the Wycliffe Bible; about 25 of these manuscripts come from the original work of 1382. The oldest known manuscript of Purvey's revision is dated 1408.

[4] Brian Edwards, *God's Outlaw* (Wheaton, Ill.: Tyndale House Publishers, 1981), 61.

[5] Ibid., 168.

[6] The Coverdale Bible was the first English Bible to be printed in England. This Bible did not include the books now known as the Apocrypha (meaning "hidden").

[7] J. H. Skilton, "English Versions of the Bible" in the *New Bible Dictionary* (Leicester, England: Inter-Varsity Press; Wheaton, Ill.: Tyndale House Publishers, 1962), 325–33.

Note: Some of the material in this chapter was adapted from an unpublished article, "The History of the English Bible," by Paul M. Bechtel for the Tyndale Encyclopedia project.

THE STORY OF THE ENGLISH BIBLE
From the King James Version to the Revised Standard Version

THE EIGHTEENTH AND NINETEENTH CENTURIES: NEW DISCOVERIES OF EARLIER MANUSCRIPTS AND INCREASED KNOWLEDGE OF THE ORIGINAL LANGUAGES

The King James Version became the most popular English translation in the seventeenth and eighteenth centuries. It acquired the stature of becoming the standard English Bible. But the King James Version had deficiencies that did not go unnoticed by certain scholars. First, knowledge of Hebrew was inadequate in the early seventeenth century. The Hebrew text they used (i.e., the Masoretic Text—see chapter 2) was adequate, but their understanding of the Hebrew vocabulary was insufficient. It would take many more years of linguistic studies to enrich and sharpen understanding of the Hebrew vocabulary. Second, the Greek text underlying the New Testament of the King James Version was an inferior text. The King James translators basically used a Greek text known as the Textus Receptus (or, the "Received Text"), which came from the work of Erasmus, who compiled the first Greek text to be produced on a printing press. When Erasmus compiled this text, he used five or six very late manuscripts dating from the tenth to the thirteenth century. These manuscripts were far inferior to earlier manuscripts.

The King James translators had done well with the resources that were available to them, but those resources were insufficient, especially with respect to the New Testament text. After the King James Version was published, earlier and better manuscripts were discovered. Around 1630, Codex Alexandrinus was brought to England. A fifth century manuscript containing the entire New Testament, it provided a good, early witness to the New Testament text, especially the original text of Revelation. Two hundred years later, a German scholar named Constantin von Tischendorf discovered Codex Sinaiticus in St. Catherine's Monastery located near Mount Sinai. The manuscript, dated around A.D. 350, is one of the two oldest vellum (treated animal hide) manuscripts of the Greek New Testament. The earliest vellum manuscript, Codex Vaticanus, had been in the Vatican's library since at least 1481, but it was not made available to scholars until the middle of the nineteenth century. This manuscript, dated slightly earlier (A.D. 325) than Codex Sinaiticus, has both the Old and New Testaments in Greek, excluding the last part of the New Testament (Hebrews 9:15 to Revelation 22:21

and the Pastoral Epistles). A hundred years of textual criticism has determined that this manuscript is one of the most accurate and reliable witnesses. Other early and important manuscripts were discovered in the nineteenth century. Through the tireless labors of men like Constantin von Tischendorf, Samuel Tregelles, and F. H. A. Scrivener, manuscripts such as Codex Ephraemi Rescriptus, Codex Zacynthius, and Codex Augiensis were deciphered, collated, and published.

As the various manuscripts were discovered and made public, certain scholars labored to compile a Greek text that would more closely represent the original text than did the Textus Receptus. Around 1700 John Mill produced an improved Textus Receptus, and in the 1730s Johannes Albert Bengel, known as the father of modern textual and philological studies in the New Testament, published a text that deviated from the Textus Receptus according to the evidence of earlier manuscripts.

In the 1800s certain scholars began to abandon the Textus Receptus. Karl Lachman, a classical philologist, produced a fresh text in 1831 that represented the fourth century manuscripts. Samuel Tregelles, self-taught in Latin, Hebrew, and Greek, laboring throughout his entire lifetime, concentrated all of his efforts in publishing one Greek text, which came out in six parts, from 1857 to 1872.[1]

His goal was "to exhibit the text of the New Testament in the very words in which it has been transmitted on the evidence of ancient authority."[2]

Henry Alford also compiled a Greek text based upon the best and earliest manuscripts. In his preface to *The Greek New Testament,* a multi-volume commentary on the Greek New Testament, published in 1849, Alford said he labored for the "demolition of the unworthy and pedantic reverence for the received text, which stood in the way of all chance of discovering the genuine word of God."[3]

During this same year, Tischendorf was devoting a lifetime of labor to discovering manuscripts and producing accurate editions of the Greek New Testament. In a letter to his fiancée, he wrote, "I am confronted with a sacred task, the struggle to regain the original form of the New Testament."

In keeping with his desire, he discovered Codex Sinaiticus, deciphered the palimpsest[4] Codex Ephraemi Rescriptus, collated countless manuscripts, and produced several editions of the Greek New Testament (the eighth edition is the best).

Aided by the work of the previous scholars, two British men, Brooke Westcott and Fenton Hort, worked together for twenty-eight years to produce a volume entitled *The New Testament in the Original Greek* (1881). Along with this publication, they made known their theory (which was chiefly Hort's) that Codex Vaticanus and Codex Sinaiticus, along with a few other early manuscripts, represented a text that most closely replicated the original writing. They called this text the Neutral Text. (According to their studies, the Neutral Text described certain manuscripts that had the least amount of textual corruption.) This is the text that Westcott and Hort relied upon for compiling their edition called *The New Testament in the Original Greek*.

THE ENGLISH REVISED VERSION AND THE AMERICAN STANDARD VERSION

By the latter part of the nineteenth century, the Christian community had been given three very good Greek New Testament texts: Tregelles', Tischendorf's, and Westcott and Hort's. These texts were very different from the Textus Receptus. And as was mentioned earlier, the scholarly community had accumulated more knowledge about the meaning of various Hebrew words and Greek words. Therefore, there was a great need for a new English translation based upon a better text— and with more accurate renderings of the original languages.

A few individuals attempted to meet this need. In 1871 John Nelson Darby, leader of the Plymouth

Brethren movement, produced a translation called the *New Translation,*) which was largely based on Codex Vaticanus and Codex Sinaiticus. In 1872 J. B. Rotherham published a translation of Tregelles' text, in which he attempted to reflect the emphasis inherent in the Greek text. This translation is still being published under the title *The Emphasized Bible*. And in 1875 Samuel Davidson produced a New Testament translation of Tischendorf's text.

The first major corporate effort was initiated in 1870 by the Convocation of Canterbury, which decided to sponsor a major revision of the King James Version. Sixty-five British scholars, working in various committees, made significant changes in the King James Version. The Old Testament scholars corrected mistranslations of Hebrew words and reformatted poetic passages into poetic form. The New Testament scholars made thousands of changes based upon better textual evidence. Their goal was to make the New Testament revision reflect, not the Textus Receptus, but the texts of Tregelles, Tischendorf, and Westcott and Hort. When the complete Revised Version appeared in 1885, it was received with great enthusiasm. Over 3 million copies sold in the first year of its publication. Unfortunately, its popularity was not long lasting because most people continued to prefer the King James Version over all other translations.

Several American scholars had been invited to join the revision work, with the understanding that any of their suggestions not accepted by the British scholars would appear in an appendix. Furthermore, the American scholars had to agree not to publish their own American revision until after fourteen years. When the time came (1901), the American Standard Version was published by several surviving members of the original American committee. This translation, generally regarded as superior to the English Revised Version, is an accurate, literal rendering of very trustworthy texts both in the Old Testament and the New.

THE TWENTIETH CENTURY: NEW DISCOVERIES AND NEW TRANSLATIONS

The nineteenth century was a fruitful era for the Greek New Testament and subsequent English translations; it was also a century in which Hebrew studies were greatly advanced. The twentieth century has also been fruitful—especially for textual studies. Those living in the twentieth century have witnessed the discovery of the Dead Sea Scrolls (see the discussion in chapter 2), the Oxyrhynchus Papyri, the Chester Beatty Papyri, and the Bodmer Papyri (see the discussion in chapter 3). These amazing discoveries, providing scholars with hundreds of ancient manuscripts, have greatly enhanced the effort to recover the original wording of the Old and New Testaments. At the same time, other archaeological discoveries have validated the historical accuracy of the Bible and helped Bible scholars understand the meaning of certain ancient words. For example, the Greek word *parousia* (usually translated "coming") was found in many ancient documents dated around the time of Christ; very often the word indicated the visitation of royalty. When this word was used in the New Testament concerning Christ's second coming, the readers would think of his coming as being the visitation of a king. In Koine Greek, the expression *entos humon* (literally, "inside of you") often meant "within reach." Thus, Jesus' statement in Luke 17:21 could mean, "The kingdom is within reach."

As earlier and better manuscripts of the Bible have emerged, scholars have been engaged in updating the Bible texts. Old Testament scholars have still used the Masoretic Text but have noted significant differences found in the Dead Sea Scrolls. The current edition used by Old Testament scholars is called *Biblia Hebraica Stuttgartensia*. New Testament scholars, for the most part, have come to rely upon the an edition of the Greek New Testament known as the Nestle-Aland text. Eberhard Nestle used the best editions of the Greek

New Testament produced in the nineteenth century to compile a text that represented the majority consensus.[5] The work of making new editions was carried on by his son for several years and is now under the care of Kurt Aland. The latest edition (the 26th) of Nestle-Aland's *Novum Testamentum Graece* appeared in 1979, with a corrected edition in 1986. The same Greek text appears in another popular volume published by the United Bible Societies, called the *Greek New Testament* (3d, corrected ed.—1983).

EARLY TWENTIETH CENTURY TRANSLATIONS IN THE LANGUAGE OF THE PEOPLE

The thousands and thousands of papyri that were discovered in Egypt around the turn of the century displayed a form of Greek called "koine" Greek. Koine (meaning "common") Greek was everyman's Greek; it was the common language of almost everybody living in Graeco-Roman world from the second century B.C. to the third century A.D. In other words, it was the "lingua franca" of the Mediterranean world. Every educated person back then could speak, read, and write in Greek just like every educated person in modern times can speak a little English, read some English, and perhaps write in English. Koine Greek was not literary Greek (i.e., the kind of Greek written by the Greek poets and tragedians); it was the kind of Greek used in personal letters, legal documents, and other non-literary texts.

New Testament scholars began to discover that most of the New Testament was written in Koine Greek—the language of the people.[6] As a result, there was a strong prompting to translate the New Testament into the language of the people. Various translators chose to divorce themselves from the traditional Elizabethan English as found in the King James Version (and even in the English Revised Version and American Standard Version) and produce fresh renderings in the common idiom.

THE TWENTIETH CENTURY NEW TESTAMENT

The first of these new translations was *The Twentieth Century New Testament* (1902). The preface to a new edition of this translation provides an excellent description of the work:

> *The Twentieth Century New Testament* is a smooth-flowing, accurate, easy-to-read translation that captivates its readers from start to finish. Born out of a desire to make the Bible readable and understandable, it is the product of the labors of a committee of twenty men

and women who worked together over ma
years to construct, we believe under divine
surveillance, this beautifully simple rendition
of the Word of God.[7]

THE NEW TESTAMENT IN MODERN SPEECH

A year after the publication of *The Twentieth Century New Testament,* Richard Weymouth published *The New Testament in Modern Speech* (1903). Weymouth, who had received the first Doctor of Literature degree from the University of London, was a headmaster of a private school in London. During his life, he spent time producing an edition of the Greek text (published in 1862) that was more accurate than the Textus Receptus, and then he labored to produce an English translation of this Greek text (called *The Resultant Greek Testament*) in a modern speech version. His translation was very well received; it has gone through several editions and many printings.

THE NEW TESTAMENT: A NEW TRANSLATION

Another new and fresh translation to appear in the early years of this century was one written by James Moffatt, a brilliant Scottish scholar. In 1913 he published his first edition of *The New Testament:*

A New Translation. This was actually his second translation of the New Testament; his first was done in 1901, called *The Historical New Testament.* In his *New Translation* Moffatt's goal was "to translate the New Testament exactly as one would render any piece of contemporary Hellenistic prose." His work displays brilliance and marked independence from other versions; unfortunately it was based on Hermann von Soden's Greek New Testament, which, as all scholars now know, is quite defective.

THE COMPLETE BIBLE: AN AMERICAN TRANSLATION

The earliest American modern speech translation was produced by Edgar J. Goodspeed, a professor of New Testament at the University of Chicago. He had criticized *The Twentieth Century New Testament,* Weymouth's version, and Moffatt's translation. As a consequence, he was challenged by some other scholars to do better. He took up the challenge and in 1923 published *The New Testament: An American Translation.* When he made this translation he said that he wanted to give his "version something of the force and freshness that reside in the original Greek." He said, "I wanted my translation to make on the reader something of the impression the New Testament must have made on its earliest readers, and to invite the continuous reading of the whole book at a time."[8] His translation was a success. An Old Testament translation followed, produced by J. M. Powis Smith and three other scholars. *The Complete Bible: An American Translation* was published in 1935.

THE REVISED STANDARD VERSION

The English Revised Version and the American Standard Version had gained a reputation of being accurate study texts but very "wooden" in their construction. The translators who worked on the Revised Versions attempted to translate words consistently from the original language regardless of its context and sometimes even followed the word order of the Greek. This created a very unidiomatic version. This called for a new revision.

The demand for revision was strengthened by the fact that several important biblical manuscripts had been discovered in the 1930s and 1940s— namely, the Dead Sea Scrolls for the Old Testament and the Chester Beatty Papyri for the New Testament. It was felt that the fresh evidence displayed in these documents should be reflected in a revision. The revision showed some textual changes in the book of Isaiah due to the Isaiah scroll and several changes in the Pauline Epistles due to the Chester Beatty Papyrus, P46. There were

other significant revisions. The story of the
woman caught in adultery (John 7:52–8:11) was
not included in the text but in the margin because
none of the early manuscripts contain this story,
and the ending to Mark (16:9-20) was not included
in the text because it is not found in the two
earliest manuscripts, Codex Vaticanus and Codex
Sinaiticus.

The organization that held the copyright to the
American Standard Version, called the International
Council of Religious Education, authorized a new
revision in 1937. The New Testament translators
generally followed the seventeenth edition of the
Nestle Text (1941), while the Old Testament translators followed the Masoretic Text. Both groups, however, adopted readings from other ancient sources
when they were considered to be more accurate.
The New Testament was published in 1946, and the
entire Bible with the Old Testament, in 1952.

The principles of the revision were specified in
the preface to the Revised Standard Version:

> The Revised Standard Version is not a new
> translation in the language of today. It is not
> a paraphrase which aims at striking idioms. It
> is a revision which seeks to preserve all that is
> best in the English Bible as it as been known
> and used throughout the years.

This revision was well received by many Protestant churches and soon became their "standard" text. The Revised Standard Version was later published with the Apocrypha of the Old Testament (1957), in a Catholic Edition (1965), and in what is called the *Common Bible,* which includes the Old Testament, the New Testament, the Apocrypha, and the Deuterocanonical books, with international endorsements by Protestants, Greek Orthodox, and Roman Catholics. Evangelical and fundamental Christians, however, did not receive the Revised Standard Version very well—primarily because of one verse, Isaiah 7:14, which reads, "Therefore the Lord himself will give you a sign. Look, the young woman is with child and shall bear a son, and shall name him Immanuel." Evangelicals and fundamentalists contend that the text should read "virgin," not "young woman."[9] As a result, the Revised Standard Version was panned, if not banned, by many evangelical and fundamental Christians.

NOTES

[1]Because he was very poor, Tregelles had to ask sponsors to help him with the cost of publishing. The text came out in six volumes over a fifteen-year period—the last being completed just prior to his death. I consider myself fortunate to own a copy of Tregelles' *Greek New Testament* with his signature.

[2]Prolegomena to Tregelles' *Greek New Testament.*

[3]Prolegomena to Alford's *Greek Testament.*

[4]A palimpsest is a manuscript in which the original writing has been erased and then written over. Through the use of chemicals and painstaking effort, a scholar can read the original writing underneath the overprinted text. Tischendorf did this with a manuscript called Codex Ephraemi Rescriptus, which had the sermons of Ephraem written over a New Testament text.

[5]In *Handbook to the Textual Criticism of the New Testament* (London: Macmillan, 1901), Frederic Kenyon provided an excellent description of Nestle's text:

> His text (in its original form) is based upon the texts of Tischendorf and Westcott-Hort, and upon that produced by Mr. F. R. Weymouth (*The Resultant Greek Testament*, 1886), which is itself the result of the comparison of the texts of Stephanus, Lachmann, Tregelles, Tischendorf, Lightfoot, Ellicott, Alford, Weiss, the Basel edition of 1880, Westcott and Hort, and the Revised Version. In later editions (1901, etc.) Weiss has been substituted for Weymouth. Of these three editions, Dr. Nestle follows the verdict of the majority, placing the reading of the minority in the margin.

[6]A few books in the New Testament were written in a style closer to classical Greek than Koine Greek. Luke, himself a Greek and a physician, wrote Luke and Acts in polished Greek; and the writer of Hebrews wrote prosaic Greek.

[7]Preface to the new edition (1961) published by Moody Press.

[8]Edgar J. Goodspeed, *New Chapters in New Testament Study* (New York: Macmillan, 1937) 113.

[9]The Hebrew word for "virgin" (*lamah*) can mean a young woman engaged to be married or simply a young woman. In the Septuagint translation of Isaiah, the translator used the Greek word *parthenos* ("virgin"). Matthew must have followed the Septuagint translation, for he understood Isaiah 7:14 to be a prophetic word concerning the Virgin Mary (see Matt. 1:23).

THE STORY OF THE ENGLISH BIBLE
Modern Twentieth Century Translations

THE NEW ENGLISH BIBLE

In the year that the New Testament of the Revised Standard Version was published (1946), the Church of Scotland proposed to other churches in Great Britain that it was time for a completely new translation of the Bible to be done. Those who initiated this work asked the translators to produce a fresh translation in modern idiom of the original languages; this was not to be a revision of any foregoing translation, nor was it to be a literal translation. The translators, under the direction of C. H. Dodd, were called upon to translate the meaning of the text into modern English. The preface to the New Testament (published in 1961), written by C. H. Dodd, explains this more fully:

> The older translators, on the whole, considered that fidelity to the original demanded that they should reproduce, as far as possible, character-istic features of the language in which it was written, such as the syntactical order of words, the structure and division of sentences, and even

such irregularities of grammar as were indeed natural enough to authors writing in the easy idiom of popular Hellenistic Greek, but less natural when turned into English. The present translators were enjoined to replace Greek constructions and idioms by those of contemporary English.

This meant a different theory and practice of translation, and one which laid a heavier burden on the translators. Fidelity in translation was not to mean keeping the general framework of the original intact while replacing Greek words by English words more or less equivalent. . . . Thus we have not felt obliged (as did the Revisers of 1881) to make an effort to render the same Greek word everywhere by the same English word. We have in this respect returned to the wholesome practice of King James's men, who (as they expressly state in their preface) recognized no such obligation. We have conceived our task to be that of understanding the original as precisely as we could (using all available aids), and then saying again in our own native idiom what we believed the author to be saying in his.

The entire *New English Bible* was published in 1970; it was well-received in Great Britain and in the United States (even though its idiom is

extremely British) and was especially praised for
its good literary style. The translators were very
experimental, producing renderings never before
printed in an English version and adopting certain
readings from various Hebrew and Greek manuscripts never before adopted. As a result, *The New
English Bible* was both highly praised for its ingenu-
ity and severely criticized for its liberty.

THE GOOD NEWS BIBLE:
TODAY'S ENGLISH VERSION

The New Testament in Today's English Version,
also known as *Good News for Modern Man,* was
published by the American Bible Society in 1966.
The translation was originally done by Robert
Bratcher, a research associate of the Translations
Department of the American Bible Society, and
then further refined by the American Bible Society.
The translation, heavily promoted by several Bible
societies and very affordable, sold more than
35 million copies within six years of the time
of printing. The New Testament translation,
based upon the first edition of the *Greek New
Testament* (the United Bible Societies, 1966),
is an idiomatic version in modern and simple
English. The translation was greatly influenced
by the linguistic theory of dynamic equivalence
(see next chapter) and was quite successful

in providing English readers with a translation
that, for the most part, accurately reflects the
meaning of the original texts. This is explained in
the preface to the New Testament:

> This translation of the New Testament has been
> prepared by the American Bible Society for
> people who speak English as their mother
> tongue or as an acquired language. As a dis-
> tinctly new translation, it does not conform
> to traditional vocabulary or style, but seeks to
> express the meaning of the Greek text in words
> and forms accepted as standard by people
> everywhere who employ English as a means of
> communication. Today's English Version of the
> New Testament attempts to follow, in this century,
> the example set by the authors of the New Testa-
> ment books, who, for the most part, wrote in the
> standard, or common, form of the Greek lan-
> guage used throughout the Roman Empire.

Because of the success of the New Testament,
the American Bible Society was asked by other
Bible societies to make an Old Testament translation following the same principles used in the
New Testament. The entire Bible was published
in 1976, and is known as the *Good News Bible:*
Today's English Version.

THE LIVING BIBLE

In 1962 Kenneth Taylor published a paraphrase
of the New Testament Epistles in a volume called
Living Letters. This new dynamic paraphrase, written in common vernacular, became well received
and widely acclaimed—especially for its ability to
communicate the message of God's Word to the
common man. In the beginning its circulation was
greatly enhanced by the endorsement of the Billy
Graham Evangelistic Association, which did much
to publicize the book and distributed thousands of
free copies. Taylor continued to paraphrase other
portions of the Bible and publish successive volumes: *Living Prophecies* (1965), *Living Gospels*
(1966), *Living Psalms* (1967), *Living Lessons of
Life and Love* (1968), *Living Books of Moses*
(1969), and *Living History of Moses* (1970). The
entire *Living Bible* was published in 1971 (the
Living New Testament was printed in 1966).

Using the American Standard Version as his
working text, Taylor rephrased the Bible into
modern speech—such that anyone, even a child,
could understand the message of the original
writers. In the preface to *The Living Bible* Taylor
explains his view of paraphrasing:

> To paraphrase is to say something in different
> words than the author used. It is a restatement

of the author's thoughts, using different words than he did. This book is a paraphrase of the Old and New Testaments. Its purpose is to say as exactly as possible what the writers of the Scriptures meant, and to say it simply, expanding where necessary for a clear understanding by the modern reader.

Even though many modern readers have greatly appreciated the fact that *The Living Bible* made God's Word clear to them, Taylor's paraphrase has been criticized for being too interpretive. But that is the nature of paraphrases—and the danger as well. Taylor was aware of this when he made the paraphrase. Again, the preface clarifies:

> There are dangers in paraphrases, as well as values. For whenever the author's exact words are not translated from the original languages, there is a possibility that the translator, however honest, may be giving the English reader something that the original writer did not mean to say.

The Living Bible has been very popular among English readers worldwide. More than 35 million copies have been sold by the publishing house Taylor specifically created to publish *The Living*

Bible. The company is called Tyndale House Publishers—named after William Tyndale, the father of modern English translations of the Bible.

THE NEW AMERICAN STANDARD BIBLE

There are two modern translations that are both revisions of (or based on) the American Standard Version (1901): the Revised Standard Version (1952) and the *New American Standard Bible* (1971). The Lockman Foundation, a nonprofit Christian corporation committed to evangelism, promoted this revision of the American Standard Version because "the producers of this translation were imbued with the conviction that interest in the American Standard Version 1901 should be renewed and increased." [1] Indeed, the American Standard Version was a monumental work of scholarship and a very accurate translation. However, its popularity was waning, and it was fast disappearing from the scene. Therefore, the Lockman Foundation organized a team of thirty-two scholars to prepare a new revision. These scholars, all committed to the inspiration of Scripture, strove to produce a literal translation of the Bible in the belief that such a translation "brings the contemporary reader as close as possible to the actual wording and grammatical structure of the original writers."[2]

The translators of the *New American Standard Bible* were instructed by the Lockman Foundation "to adhere to the original languages of the Holy Scriptures as closely as possible and at the same time to obtain a fluent and readable style according to current English usage."[3] After the *New American Standard Bible* was published (1963 for the New Testament and 1971 for the entire Bible), it received a mixed response. Some critics applauded its literal accuracy, while others sharply criticized its language for hardly being contemporary or modern.

On the whole, the *New American Standard Bible* became respected as a good study Bible that accurately reflects the wording of the original languages yet is not a good translation for Bible reading. Furthermore, it must be said that this translation is now nearly thirty years behind in terms of textual fidelity—especially the New Testament, which, though it was originally supposed to follow the 23rd edition of the Nestle text, tends to follow the Textus Receptus.

THE NEW INTERNATIONAL VERSION

The New International Version is a completely new rendering of the original languages done by an international group of more than a hundred scholars.

These scholars worked many years and in several committees to produce an excellent thought-for-thought translation in contemporary English for private and public use. The New International Version is called "international" because it was prepared by distinguished scholars from English-speaking countries such as the United States, Canada, Great Britain, Australia, and New Zealand, and because "the translators sought to use vocabulary common to the major English-speaking nations of the world."[4]

The translators of the New International Version sought to make a version that was midway between a literal rendering (as in the *New American Standard Bible*) and a free paraphrase (as in *The Living Bible*). Their goal was to convey in English the thought of the original writers. This is succinctly explained in the original preface to the New Testament:

Certain convictions and aims guided the translators. They are all committed to the full authority and complete trustworthiness of the Scriptures. Therefore, their first concern was the accuracy of the translation and its fidelity to the thought of the New Testament writers. While they weighed the significance of the lexical and grammatical details of the Greek text, they have striven for more than a word-for-word translation. Because thought patterns and syntax differ from language to language, faithful communication of the meaning of the writers of the New Testament demanded frequent modifications in sentence structure and constant regard for the contextual meanings of words.

Concern for clarity of style—that it should be idiomatic without being idiosyncratic, contemporary without being dated—also motivated the translators and their consultants. They have consistently aimed at simplicity of expression, with sensitive attention to the connotation and sound of the chosen word. At the same time, they endeavored to avoid a sameness of style in order to reflect the varied styles and moods of the New Testament writers.

The New Testament of the New International Version was published in 1973, and the entire Bible, in 1978. This version has been phenomenally successful. Millions and millions of readers have adopted the New International Version as their "Bible." Since 1987 it has outsold the King James Version, the best-seller for centuries—a remarkable indication of its popularity and acceptance in the Christian community. The New International Version, sponsored by the New York Bible Society and published by Zondervan Publishers, has become a standard version used for private reading and pulpit reading in many English-speaking countries.

TWO MODERN CATHOLIC TRANSLATIONS: THE JERUSALEM BIBLE AND THE NEW AMERICAN BIBLE

In 1943 Pope Pius XII issued the famous encyclical encouraging Roman Catholics to read and study the Scriptures. At the same time, the pope recommended that the Scriptures should be translated from the original languages. Previously, all Catholic translations were based on the Latin Vulgate. This includes Knox's translation, which was begun in 1939 and published in 1944 (the New Testament) and in 1955 (the whole Bible).

The first complete Catholic Bible to be translated from the original languages is *The Jerusalem Bible*, published in England in 1966. *The Jerusalem Bible* is the English counterpart to a French translation entitled *La Bible de Jerusalem*. The French translation was "the culmination of decades of research and biblical scholarship,"[5] published by the scholars of the Dominican Biblical School of Jerusalem. This Bible, which includes the Apocrypha and Deuterocanonical books, contains many study helps—such as introductions to each book of the Bible, extensive notes on various passages, and maps. The study helps are an intricate part of the whole translation because it is the belief of Roman Catholic leadership that laypeople should be given interpretive helps in their reading of the sacred text. The study helps in *The Jerusalem Bible* were translated from the French, whereas the Bible text itself was translated from the original languages, with the help of the French translation. The translation of the text produced under the editorship of Alexander Jones is considerably freer than other translations, such as the Revised Standard Version, because the translators sought to capture the meaning of the original writings in a "vigorous, contemporary literary style."[6]

The first American Catholic Bible to be translated from the original languages is *The New American Bible* (not to be confused with the *New American Standard Bible*). Although this translation was published in 1970, work had begun on this version several decades before. Prior to Pope Pius's encyclical, an American translation of the New Testament based on the Latin Vulgate was published—known as The Confraternity Version. After the encyclical, the Old Testament was translated from the Hebrew Masoretic Text and the New Testament redone, based on the twenty-fifth edition of the Greek

Nestle-Aland text. *The New American Bible* has short introductions to each book of the Bible and very few marginal notes. Kubo and Specht provide a just description of the translation itself:

> The translation itself is simple, clear, and straightforward and reads very smoothly. It is good American English, not as pungent and colorful as the N.E.B. [*New English Bible*]. Its translations are not striking but neither are they clumsy. They seem to be more conservative in the sense that they tend not to stray from the original. That is not to say that this is a literal translation, but it is more faithful.[7]

JEWISH TRANSLATIONS

In the twentieth century some very important Jewish translations of the Bible were published. The Jewish Publication Society created a translation of the Hebrew Scriptures called *The Holy Scriptures According to the Masoretic Text, A New Translation* (published in 1917). The preface to this translation explains its purpose:

> It aims to combine the spirit of Jewish tradition with the results of biblical scholarship, ancient, medieval and modern. It gives to the Jewish world a translation of the Scriptures done

by men imbued with the Jewish consciousness, while the non-Jewish world, it is hoped, will welcome a translation that presents many passages from the Jewish traditional point of view.

In 1955 the Jewish Publication Society appointed a new committee of seven eminent Jewish scholars to make a new Jewish translation of the Hebrew Scriptures. The translation called The New Jewish Version was published in 1962. A second, improved edition was published in 1973. This work is not a revision of *The Holy Scriptures According to the Masoretic Text*; it is a completely new translation in modern English. The translators attempted "to produce a version that would carry the same message to modern man as the original did to the world of ancient times."[8]

REVISIONS, REVISIONS, REVISIONS

The last part of the twentieth century (the 1980s and 1990s) seems to be a time for new revisions, not new translations. The general consensus among the consumers is, "We have enough translations, don't give us any more." Most of the publishers seem to be getting the message. Therefore, instead of publishing new translations, they are issuing new, revised editions of existing translations.

The New Revised Standard Version published in 1990 is an excellent example of this current trend. In the preface to this revision, Bruce Metzger, chairperson of the revision committee, wrote:

> The New Revised Standard Version of the Bible is an authorized revision of the Revised Standard Version, published in 1952, which was a revision of the American Standard Version, published in 1901, which, in turn, embodied earlier revisions of the King James Version, published in 1611.
>
> The need for issuing a revision of the Revised Standard Version of the Bible arises from three circumstances: (a) the acquisition of still older Biblical manuscripts, (b) further investigation of linguistic features of the text, and (c) changes in preferred English usage.

The three criteria specified by Metzger for the New Revised Standard Version are essentially the same principles behind all revisions of Bible translations.

In the 1980s several significant revisions appeared: the New King James Version (1982); *The New Jerusalem Bible* (1986); *The New American Bible,* Revised New Testament (1986); and the *Revised English Bible* (1989), which is a radical revision of the *New English Bible*. Other translations, such as the New International Version and Today's English Version, were also revised in 1980s but not publicized as such. Inevitably, more revisions, and perhaps some new translations, will appear in the 1990s.

NOTES

[1]From the Preface to the *New American Standard Bible*.
[2]Ibid.
[3]Sakae Kubo and Walter Specht, *So Many Versions?* rev. ed. (Grand Rapids, Mich.: Zondervan, 1983), 171.
[4]Ibid., 191–92.
[5]From the Preface to the *New Jerusalem Bible*.
[6]Ibid.
[7]Kubo and Specht, *Versions*, 165.
[8]Ibid., 108.

WHY SO MANY TRANSLATIONS?
A Look at Different Ways of Translating the Bible

As mentioned in the Introduction, when I teach New Testament Literature and Interpretation at Wheaton College, I always give lectures about the history of the English Bible and about the various modern translations that are available to English readers. I believe it is important for students living in an age where there is a plethora of translations to know something about each one.

When I give my lectures, I am often asked, "Which translation is the best?" Invariably I respond, "Best for what? For reading? For studying? For memorizing? And best for whom? For young people? For adults? For Protestants? For Catholics? For Jews?" My responses are not intended to be complicated; rather, they reflect the complexity of the true situation. Whereas for some language populations, there is only one translation of the Bible, English-speaking people have hundreds of translations. Therefore, one cannot say there is *one* single *best* translation that is *the most* accurate. Accuracy of translation must be assessed in terms of the kind of translation being judged. The same criteria cannot be used for a literal translation and an idiomatic translation.

TRYING TO DEFINE "TRANSLATION"

There are two basic theories and/or methodologies of Bible translation. The first has been called "Formal Equivalence." According to this theory, the translator attempts to render the exact words (hence the word *formal*—form for form, or word for word) of the original language into the receptor language. The second has been called "dynamic equivalence" by the eminent translation theorist Eugene Nida. He has defined the ideal of translation as "the reproduction in a receptor language [i.e., English] of the closest natural equivalent of the source language [i.e., Hebrew or Greek] message, first in terms of meaning, and second in terms of style."[1] Nida, therefore, believes that a translation should have the same dynamic impact upon modern readers as the original had upon its audience. He elaborates on this as follows:

> Dynamic equivalence is therefore to be defined
> in terms of the degree to which the receptors
> of the message in the receptor language respond
> to it in substantially the same manner as
> the receptors in the source language. This

response can never be identical, for the
cultural and historical settings are too different,
but there should be a high degree of equivalence of response, or the translation will have
failed to accomplish its purpose.[2]

Nida's theory of dynamic equivalence has
become a standard or ideal that many modern
translators have attempted to attain. Goodspeed
expressed this desire about his *American
Translation* when he said, "I wanted my translation to make on the reader something of the
impression the New Testament must have made
on its earliest readers."[3] Another way of speaking
about a dynamic equivalent translation is to
call it a thought-for-thought translation (as opposed
to a word-for-word). Of course, to translate
the thought of the original language requires
that the text be interpreted accurately and
then rendered in understandable idiom. Thus,
the goal of any dynamic equivalent translation
is for it to be exegetically accurate and idiomatically
powerful.

A good translation must be reliable and
readable—that is, it must reliably replicate the
meaning of the text without sacrificing its readability. At various points in the Scriptures, there
is evidence that the biblical documents were

written to be read aloud, usually in public worship (see Nehemiah 8; Luke 4:16-17; 1 Timothy 4:13; Revelation 1:3). Undoubtedly those ancient hearers of the Word understood the message as it was delivered to them. Any translation should be just as fluent and intelligible to a modern audience. This, of course, does not mean that translation can replace inter-pretation of difficult passages, as in the case of the eunuch who needed Philip's interpretation of Isaiah 53 (see Acts 8:28-35); but a good rendering minimizes the need for unnecessary exegesis (a technical term used by Bible scholars for "drawing out the meaning of the text").

Ever since the time of Jerome, who produced the translation known as the Latin Vulgate, there has been a debate over what is the best method to translate the Bible: the word-for-word approach or the sense-for-sense. In a letter to a person called Pammachius, Jerome exhibited this tension when he wrote:

> For I myself not only admit but freely pro-claim that in translating from the Greek (except in the case of the holy scriptures where even the order of the words is a mystery) I render sense for sense and not word for word.[4]

When it came to translating the Scriptures, Jerome, contrary to his normal practice, felt the compulsion to render word for word; but, as is well known, he did not always do so in the Vulgate. Yet very few would now demand it of him because most agree that strict literalism can greatly distort the original meaning.

Martin Luther, the great reformer and translator of the German Bible, believed that a translator's paramount task was to reproduce the spirit of the author; at times this could only be accomplished by an idiomatic rendering, though when the original required it, word for word was to be used.[5] Other translators have preferred to be very literal because they feared that in translating on a thought-for-thought basis they might alter the text according to their own subjective inter-pretation. Indeed, it is true that a word-for-word rendering can be executed more easily than a thought-for-thought one; for in doing the latter, the translator must enter into the same thought as the author—and who can always know with certainty what the author's original, intended meaning was? Therefore, a dynamic-equivalent or thought-for-thought translation should be done by a group of scholars (to guard against personal subjectivism), who employ the best exegetical tools. In this regard, Beekman and Callow give excellent advice:

> Translating faithfully involves knowing what Scripture means. This is fundamental to all idiomatic translation, and it is at this point that exegesis comes in. Toussaint, in an article in *Notes on Translation*, defines exegesis as follows: "Exegesis is a critical study of the Bible according to hermeneutical principles with the immediate purpose of interpreting the text." In other words, its immediate purpose is to ascertain, as accurately as possible, using all the means available, just what the original writer, "moved by the Holy Spirit," meant as he dictated or penned his words, phrases, and sentences. Exegesis thus lies at the heart of all translation work, for if the translator does not know what the original means, then it is impossible for him to translate faithfully.[6]

The analysis of the modern translations of the prologue to John's Gospel (in the next chapter) will demonstrate how important exegesis is to translation. Major differences in translation come from major differences in interpretation.

COMPARING THE MODERN TRANSLATIONS

Each of the modern translations that was discussed in the previous chapters was based on a particular philosophy of translation. For example, the Revised Standard Version and the *New American Standard Bible,* which share a common purpose (i.e., to revise and revive the American Standard Version), are more literal than most versions. The translators often adhered to a word-for-word methodology instead of a thought-for-thought. The New Revised Standard Version is a little more "free"; in fact, the guiding concept for this revision was "as literal as possible, as free as necessary." The New International Version is even more free than The New Revised Standard Version because the translators employed a thought-for-thought approach to translation. And yet the New International Version is not as free as Today's English Version, the *New Jerusalem Bible,* and the *Revised English Bible* because these versions were created to be as contemporary as possible. Of course, these are generalized observations; such exact distinctions between the translations cannot always be so clearly delineated. At times, the translations will cross over these boundaries. Nonetheless, it is possible to classify several of the modern translations as follows:

STRICTLY LITERAL:
New American Standard Bible

LITERAL:
New King James Version
Revised Standard Version
New American Bible

LITERAL WITH FREEDOM TO BE IDIOMATIC:
New Revised Standard Version

THOUGHT-FOR-THOUGHT:
New International Version
New Jerusalem Bible
Revised English Bible
New Jewish Version

DYNAMIC EQUIVALENT (MODERN SPEECH):
Today's English Version

PARAPHRASTIC:
The Living Bible

A modern English reader (or student) of the Bible would do well to use five or six translations—one in each category listed above. For example, I use the *New American Standard Bible* and the New Revised Standard Version for detailed word studies, the New International Version and *New Jerusalem Bible* for general study, and *The Living Bible* for reading pleasure. Other readers would make different selections from the various categories, depending on their needs and preferences. Those who use one translation exclusively would be enriched if they used a few others. This is especially true for those who are King James Version enthusiasts. They would discover that their Bible reading would be infused with fresh life and new light if they read a modern version.

In selecting a translation of the Bible, the consumer should always make sure that the translation was based on the latest, most authoritative texts. Preferably, the Old Testament should have basically followed *Biblia Hebraica Stuttgartensia* and the New Testament, the United Bible Societies' third edition of the *Greek New Testament*. Many of the modern versions reflect these standard texts; whereas translations such as the King James Version and even the New King James are based on an inferior Greek text.

Finally, it must always be remembered that translations are nothing more than translations; they are not the same as the Bible in the original languages. Not one translation has been "inspired" by God in the same way the original text was. For those who want to read the Bible as it is in the original, inspired languages, they should learn Hebrew, Aramaic, and Greek. Those who do not learn these languages have to depend on translations. I can read the New Testament in Greek, but I cannot read the Old Testament in Hebrew. I have to rely on various translations of the Old Testament. Notice I used the plural, "translations," not the singular, because I believe it is imperative for modern English readers to use several of the available English versions. By using different translations the reader can acquire a fuller understanding of the meaning of the original text.

NOTES

[1]Eugene Nida and Charles Taber, *The Theory and Practice of Translation* (Leiden: E. J. Brill, 1969), 210.
[2]Ibid., 24.
[3]Edgar J. Goodspeed, *New Chapters in New Testament Study* (New York: Macmillan, 1937), 113.
[4]*The Nicene and Post Nicene Fathers,* 2d ser., vol. 6, *St. Jerome, Select Works and Letters,* trans. W. H. Fremantle; ed. Philip Schaff and Henry Wace (New York: Charles Scribner's Sons, 1912), 113.
[5]W. Schwarz, *Principles and Problems of Biblical Translation* (Cambridge: Cambridge University Press, 1955), 205–6.
[6]John Beekman and John Callow, *Translating the Word of God* (Grand Rapids, Mich.: Zondervan, 1974), 34–35.

A COMPARATIVE STUDY OF MODERN TRANSLATIONS
The Prologue to the Gospel of John

TYNDALE'S VERSION

In the beginnynge was the worde, and the worde was with God: and the word was God. The same was in the beginnynge with God. All things were made by it, and with out it, was made nothinge, that was made. In it was lyfe, and the lyfe was the lyghte of men, and the lyght shyneth in the darcknes, but the darckness comprehended it not.

KING JAMES VERSION

[1]In the beginning was the Word, and the Word was with God, and the Word was God. [2]The same was in the beginning with God. [3]All things were made by him; and without him was not any thing made that was made. [4]In him was life; and the life was the light of men. [5]And the light shineth in darkness; and the darkness comprehended it not.

AMERICAN STANDARD VERSION

[1]In the beginning was the Word, and the Word was with God, and the Word was God. [2]The same was in the beginning with God. [3]All things were made through him; and without him was not anything made that hath been made. [4]In him was life; and the life was the light of men. [5]And the light shineth in the darkness; and the darkness apprehended it not.

REVISED STANDARD VERSION
[1]In the beginning was the Word, and the Word was with God, and the Word was God. [2]He was in the beginning with God; [3]all things were made through him; and without him was not anything made that was made. [4]In him was life, and the life was the light of men. [5]The light shines in the darkness, and the darkness has not overcome it.

NEW AMERICAN STANDARD BIBLE
[1]In the beginning was the Word, and the Word was with God, and the Word was God.
[2]He was in the beginning with God.
[3]All things came into being by Him, and apart from Him nothing came into being that has come into being.
[4]In Him was life, and the life was the light of men.
[5]And the light shines in the darkness, and the darkness did not comprehend it.

NEW INTERNATIONAL VERSION
[1]In the beginning was the Word, and the Word was with God, and the Word was God. [2]He was with God in the beginning.
[3]Through him all things were made; without him nothing was made that has been made. [4]In him was life, and that life was the light of men. [5]The light shines in the darkness, but the darkness has not understood it.

TODAY'S ENGLISH VERSION

[1] Before the world was created, the Word already existed; he was with God, and he was the same as God. [2] From the very beginning the Word was with God. [3] Through him God made all things; not one thing in all creation was made without him. [4] The Word was the source of life, and this life brought light to mankind. [5] The light shines in the darkness, and the darkness has never put it out.

THE LIVING BIBLE

[1-2] Before anything else existed, there was Christ, with God. He has always been alive and is himself God. [3] He created everything there is—nothing exists that he didn't make. [4] Eternal life is in him, and this life gives light to all mankind. [5] His life is the light that shines through the darkness—and the darkness can never extinguish it.

NEW ENGLISH BIBLE

When all things began, the Word already was. The Word dwelt with God, and what God was, the Word was. The Word, then, was with God at the beginning, and through him all things came to be; no single thing was created without him. All that came to be was alive with his life, and that life was the light of men. The light shines on in the dark, and the darkness has never mastered it.

THE NEW JERUSALEM BIBLE

1   In the beginning was the Word:
the Word was with God
and the Word was God.

2   He was with God in the beginning.

3   Through him all things came into being,
not one thing came into being except through him.

4   What has come into being in him was life,
life that was the light of men;

5   and light shines in darkness,
and darkness could not overpower it.

THE NEW AMERICAN BIBLE

1   In the beginning was the Word,
and the Word was with God,
and the Word was God.

2   He was in the beginning with God.

3   All things came to be through him,
and without him nothing came to be.
What came to be [4]through him was life,
and this life was the light of the human race;

5   the light shines in the darkness,
and the darkness has not overcome it.

NEW REVISED STANDARD VERSION

[1]In the beginning was the Word, and the Word was with God, and the Word was God. [2]He was in the beginning with God. [3]All things came into being through him, and without him not one thing came into being. What has come into being [4]in him was life, and the life was the light of all people. [5]The light shines in the darkness, and the darkness did not overcome it.

A comparative study of an intriguing passage like the prologue to John's Gospel set forth in several modern translations will help focus and substantiate all the foregoing discussions about how the translations differ. By doing this study one can see which translations tend to be literal, which tend to be more idiomatic, and which are dynamically equivalent; at the same time, one can see why each translation has its own strengths and weaknesses. It takes several translations to bring out the fullness and richness of the original language—and even then, at times, all of the translations fail to convey the full meaning of the original words.

The following analysis is detailed and, at times, complex because the analysis assesses translations of the Greek text and therefore makes constant reference to Greek words. The serious reader will be rewarded if he or she works through this chapter carefully. Having done this portion of the Bible, one can go on to do comparative studies of other portions. I would recommend that the serious reader use an interlinear Hebrew and/or Greek text. The most up-to-date Hebrew-English interlinear is the

NIV Interlinear Hebrew-English Old Testament (trans. John Kohlenberger), and the most up-to-date Greek-English interlinear is *The New Greek-English Interlinear New Testament* (trans. Robert Brown and Philip Comfort; ed. J. D. Douglas). Using an interlinear with lexicons and other modern translations, a serious Bible reader can do a very thorough and enlightening study of any portion of the Bible.

ABBREVIATIONS USED IN THIS STUDY:

RSV	Revised Standard Version
NRSV	New Revised Standard Version
NEB	*New English Bible*
NEB	*Revised English Bible*
NASB	*New American Standard Bible*
NIV	New International Version
TEV	*Good News Bible:* Today's English Version

A COMPARATIVE STUDY OF JOHN 1:1-18 (THE PROLOGUE)

1:1a In the beginning was the Word, (RSV, NASB, NIV)

When all things began, the Word already was (NEB)

> Before the world was created, the Word
> already existed. (TEV)

From the outset the reader of John's Gospel is confronted with an enigmatic phrase, which in a word-for-word rendering becomes, "In the beginning was the Word." The phrase "In the beginning" most likely indicates the beginning before all beginnings, prior to the beginning of Genesis 1:1; it speaks of that eternal beginning in which the eternal Word existed. The NEB and TEV, understanding the phrase to have temporal significance, however, make this beginning equal to the beginning in Genesis 1:1. The paraphrases in the NEB and TEV might alarm the careful reader because, although their renderings indicate that the Word existed prior to Creation, they do not convey the idea that the Word existed from the beginning or from all eternity—which is the meaning probably intended by John.

All five versions render the Greek word *logos* as "the Word." There is probably no better term, although "the Expression" might suffice because the Word was the expression of God. But it is probably best to retain "the Word" because it has become a traditional title of the Son of God before his incarnation, and it will probably remain a constant expression in English translations.

1:1b and the Word was with God, (RSV, NASB, NIV)

The Word dwelt with God, (NEB)

he was with God, (TEV)

The rendering of this phrase depends upon how the Greek preposition *pros* is understood in this context. In classical usage, *pros* used in relationship between two people means "having regard to," and indicates "devotion."[1] Perhaps, John intended to convey this meaning; but it is more likely that *pros* is to be understood accord-ing to Koine usage. In Koine, *pros* (short for *prosopon pros prosopon,* "face to face") was used to show personal relationships.[2] Accordingly, two other translations, those of Williams and of Montgomery, rendered this passage, "and the Word was face to face with God." The NEB comes the closest to transferring this sense by adding "dwelt," and the REB is even better: "the Word was in God's presence." The translation "with" in the other four translations is accurate but colorless.

1:1c and the Word was God. (RSV, NASB, NIV)

and what God was, the Word was. (NEB)

and he was the same as God. (TEV)

The Greek clause underlying these translations stipulates, according to a rule of grammar, that *logos* (the Word) is the subject and *theos* (God) is the predicate nominative. Another particularity of Greek is that the article is often used for defining individual identity and is thus absent for the purpose of ascribing quality or character. In the previous clause ("the Word was with God"), there is an article before God (*ton theon*)—pointing to God the Father. In this clause, there is no article before "God." The distinction may indicate that John did not want the reader to think the Son was the Father—but the same as the Father: that is, both are "God." The NEB reads, "and what God was, the Word was,"[3] and the TEV reads, "and he was the same as God." It can be argued, however, that the grammar (a predicate nominative without an article preceding the verb and subject) simply indicates that the clause should be translated as in the RSV, NASB, and NIV: "the Word was God."

> **1:2** He was in the beginning with God; (RSV, NASB—with different punctuation)
>
> He was with God in the beginning. (NIV)
>
> The Word, then, was with God at the beginning, (NEB)

From the very beginning the Word was with God. (TEV)

The first verse establishes three separate facts: (1) the Word was in the beginning, (2) the Word was with God, and (3) the Word was God. The second verse, picking up from the third statement, joins facts two and one: the Word (who was God) was in the beginning with God. All five versions, given their minor variations, convey this. Nevertheless, it seems odd that the NEB and TEV would here use "at the beginning" or "from the very beginning" when in the first verse they paraphrased the phrase. Consistency would help the reader observe John's intended redundancy.

1:3a All things were made through him (RSV)

All things came into being by Him; (NASB)

and through him all things came to be; (NEB)

Through him all things were made; (NIV)

Through him God made all things; (TEV)

The NASB's rendering, "all things were made by him," is unfortunate because the English preposition *by* in this context connotes authorship. The Word was not the author of creation (i.e., the Creator) but the agent of creation. This agency or instrumentality is expressed in Greek by the preposition *dia*, best translated into English as "through."

Three of the translations (NRSV, NASB, NEB) have a literal rendering of the Greek verb *egeneto* (came into being or came to be); such expressions are perhaps more suggestive of creation than "made."

1:3b-4a and without him was not anything made that was made. In him was life, (RSV)

and apart from Him nothing came into being that has come into being. In Him was life; (NASB)

without him nothing was made that has been made. In him was life, (NIV)

not one thing in all creation was made without him. The Word was the source of life, (TEV)

no single thing was created without him. All that came to be was alive with his life, (NEB)

The variation in punctuation among the translations in verses 3 and 4 is due to a textual problem. The last phrase in verse 3 of the RSV has been placed with either verse 3 or verse 4 in the different versions by means of punctuation. The earliest manuscripts (the Bodmer Papyri—P66 and P75, Codex Sinaiticus, Codex Alexandrinus, Codex Vaticanus) do not have any punctuation in these verses. P75 was later corrected, as was Codex Sinaiticus. In P75 a punctuation mark was placed before the phrase, as in (1) below; in Codex Sinaiticus after it, as in (2) below:

(1) and without him was not anything created. That which was created in him was life, . . .

(2) and without him was not anything created that was created. In him was life,

The majority of the early church fathers interpreted John 1:3-4 according to the phrasing in (1). The passage was taken to mean that all created things were life by virtue of being in him (i.e., in Christ). The statement was somehow supposed to affirm that the Word (Christ) not only created the universe, he now sustains it. Interpretation changed after some Gnostic heretics used the passage to say that the Holy Spirit was "a created thing." All the fathers then shifted to the phrasing in (2). Most exegesis has followed this up until the present.

1:4 In Him was life, and the life was the light of men. (RSV, NASB)

In him was life, and that life was the light of men. (NIV)

The Word was the source of life, and this life brought light to mankind. (TEV)

All that came to be was alive with his life, and that life was the light of men. (NEB)

Having discussed the punctuation problem, let us examine other aspects of this verse. "In him was life" is a good, literal translation; but the TEV differs. Its first edition reads, "The Word had life in himself," but the third edition has, "The Word was the source of life." The first rendering is a paraphrase of John 5:26 and conveys the thought that life was located in the Word. The revision, an improvement, suggests that the Word is the source from which men can obtain life. Although this is in accord with the total thought of John's Gospel, it perhaps goes beyond what John intended here.

The second part of this verse, when rendered literally, is clear enough. Most readers will recognize that the life was the light *for* men; but the TEV removes any uncertainty.

1:5 The light shines in the darkness, and the darkness has not overcome it. (RSV)

The light shines in the darkness, and the darkness did not comprehend it. (NASB)

The light shines in the darkness, but the darkness has not understood it. (NIV)

The light shines in the darkness, and the darkness has never put it out. (TEV)

The light shines on in the dark, and the darkness has never quenched it [mastered it, 2d ed.]. (NEB)

All the versions read the same in the first clause except the NEB. The translation "shines on" seems correctly to capture the time element of verse 5 in conjunction with the sequence of verses 1-5. Since verses 1-2 deal with the eternal preexistence of the Word, they are prior to the time of Creation. Verse 3 involves the Creation; and verse 4 indicates the time period in which the Word was incarnate among men as "the light of life." Verse 5 then suggests that the light kept on shining, even after his departure.

In this second clause, the versions vary as to the translation of the predicate because the Greek

word *lambano* can mean either "lay hold of,
grasp, apprehend, comprehend", or "overcome,
overpower." This Greek verb is used quite often
in the New Testament to indicate obtainment or
appre-hension (see Acts 4:13; 10:34; Romans
9:30; 1 Corinthians 9:24; Ephesians 3:18;
Philippians 3:12-13). However, when the New
Testament elsewhere has this word in relationship
to darkness, the sense required is "overtake"
or "overcome" (see John 12:35; 1 Thessalonians
5:4). It might be that John had both meanings
in mind. He could have been asserting that the
light keeps on shining because the darkness
did not overtake it (as in the RSV, TEV, NEB); and
he could have also been decrying the fact that the
darkness (i.e., unenlightened humanity) did not
apprehend or comprehend this light (as in the
NASB, NIV). The remainder of the prologue and
even the entire Gospel underscores this sense of
misapprehension and rejection.

1:6-8 There was a man sent from God,
whose name was John. He came for
a testimony, to bear witness to the light,
that all might believe through him.
He was not the light, but came to bear
witness to the light. (RSV—and essentially NASB, NIV)

> There appeared a man named John,
> sent from God; he came as a witness to
> testify to the light, that all might become
> believers through him. He was not himself
> the light; he came to bear witness to the
> light. (NEB)

> God sent his messenger, a man named
> John, who came to tell people about the
> light, so that all should hear the message
> and believe. He himself was not the light;
> he came to tell about the light. (TEV)

Given their minor semantic and syntactic variations,
all five versions of this passage convey essentially
the same message. The most notable differences are
seen in the diverse renderings of the Greek verb
marturo. The RSV, NASB, and NIV translate it "bear
witness"—a somewhat outdated and/or religious
expression that might bewilder the reader unfamiliar with its biblical usage. In the NRSV the expression is "came as a witness to testify." "Testify" (NEB)
is more modern and more comprehensive; "tell"
(TEV), while easy to understand, fails to convey the
notion of verification and substantiation.

1:9 The true light that enlightens every man
was coming into the world; (RSV)

> The true light that gives light to every man
> was coming into the world. (NIV)

> There was the true light which, coming
> into the world, enlightens every man.
> (NASB)

> The real light which enlightens every man
> was even then coming into the world. (NEB)

> This was the real light—the light that
> comes into the world and shines on all
> mankind. (TEV)

It should be noted that all the translations except
the RSV have provided an alternative rendering in
the margin because, according to the grammar of
this sentence, the verse can be constructed in two
ways: (1) "the true light that gives light to every
man was coming into the world," or (2) "He was
the true light that gives light to every man coming
into the world." According to the Greek, the partici-
ple for "coming" can agree with either "man" or
"light"; and though "man" is closer to "coming" in
the sentence, the next verses suggest that John was
speaking of how the light came into the world.
Thus, all the translations have selected the first
rendering and relegated the second to the margin.

1:10 He was in the world, and the world was made through him, yet the world knew him not; (RSV, and essentially NASB and NIV; the NIV uses "recognize" in place of "knew")

He was in the world; but the world, though it owed its being to him, did not recognize him. (NEB)

The Word was in the world and though God made the world through him, yet the world did not recognize him. (TEV)

Since the understood subject of this verse is "the Word," the TEV supplies it. All the translations except the NEB correctly indicate that the world was made through him—a repetition of verse 3 (but observe the inconsistency in the NEB and NASB between "came into being" in verse 3 and "made" in this verse). The NEB's rendering ("the world owed its being to him") means that the world was indebted to the Word for its existence; but this does not, in and of itself, necessarily indicate that Creation has occurred through his agency. Thus, Creation is obscured, as well as the Word's instrumentality in it.

In English, "recognize" (in NEB, TEV, NIV) is more poignant than "know" (RSV, NASB), which is a general term, especially in this context. After the Word's incarnation, mankind should have recognized the one through whom they were created, but they failed to do so.

> **1:1** He came to his own home, and his own people received him not. (RSV)
>
> He came to His own, and those who were His own did not receive Him. (NASB)
>
> He came to that which was his own, but his own did not receive him. (NIV)
>
> He entered into his own realm, and his own would not receive him. (NEB)
>
> He came to his own country, but his own people did not receive him. (TEV)

The Greek idiom *ta idia* (literally, "one's own things") can designate one's own possession or domain (see NASB's footnote), but John seems to use it to designate domain (see John 16:32 and 19:27). Three versions (RSV, NEB, TEV) attempt to convey this in English by the phrases, "own home," "own realm," or "own country," respectively, while the other two leave it ambiguous (although NASB has a note). The idiom *hoi idioi* denotes "one's own people"; and, again, the RSV, NEB, and TEV make this explicit, while the NASB and NIV leave it implicit.

1:12 But to all who received him, who believed in his name, he gave power to become children of God; (RSV)

But as many as received Him, to them He gave the right to become children of God, even to those who believe in His name, (NASB)

Yet to all who received him, to those who believed in his name, he gave the right to become children of God— (NIV)

But to all who did receive him, to those who have yielded him their allegiance, he gave the right to become children of God, (NEB)

Some, however, did receive him and believed in him; so he gave them the right to become God's children. (TEV)

The Greek word rendered "receive" in this verse conveys the dual idea of admission and apprehension. In English, one possible meaning of receive is "to permit to enter," and another is "to accept as true," which is related to the idea of believing.[4] All of the translations except the NASB rearrange the original syntax by joining the third clause to the first in order to show the association between receiving and believing. Reception is dependent upon and concurrent with belief: to believe is to receive. And to believe in Christ, according to John, means more than to "have yielded him allegiance" (NEB)—which sounds like a pledge of loyalty. (This has been corrected in the REB: "those who put their trust in him.")

To those who believed in Christ, "he" (God or Christ?) gave them "the right" or "the privilege" to become the children of God. The Greek word underlying "right" or "privilege" (*exousia*) usually is translated "authority" in the New Testament; but in this context "right" is more natural. To translate it "power," as in the RSV, would require the Greek word to have been *dunamis,* a word that John never uses.

> **1:13** who were born, not of blood nor of the will of the flesh nor of the will of man, but of God (RSV, NASB—with different punctuation)
>
> children born not of natural descent, nor of human decision or a husband's will, but born of God (NIV)

> not born of any human stock, or by the fleshly
> ["physical" in REB] desire of a human father,
> but the offspring of God himself (NEB)

> They did not become God's children by
> natural means, that is, by being born as the
> children of a human father; God himself
> was their Father (TEV)

In this verse John wanted to make it emphatically
clear that becoming a child of God necessitates
divine generation and no other kind. Using four
prepositional phrases, each beginning with the
Greek preposition *ek* (which denotes source), he
thrice states what the origin of this birth is not and
once states what the origin is. There is substantial
variation among the versions as to how to translate
these four prepositional phrases. The first prepositional phrase (literally, "not from bloods") comes
from a Hebrew idiom that indicates physical generation. Most commentators take this to mean natural
descent, perhaps with reference to Abraham's lin-
eage; thus, one is not a child of God because his
genealogy traces to Abraham. At any rate, the RSV
and NASB render this phrase almost literally, while
the NIV, TEV, and NEB translate it idiomatically.

The second phrase (literally, "not from the will
[or desire] of the flesh") has been interpreted by

some as implying sexual desire. Others, understanding the Greek word for "flesh" to designate that which is human, think this phrase signifies human volition. Again, the RSV and NASB avoid making an exegetical commitment by translating literally. The NEB appropriates the meaning of sexual desire; the NIV, on the other hand, takes the phrase to suggest human volition. Because the TEV translators understood "the last two phrases as equivalent, the one qualifying the other,"[5] the TEV collapses this phrase into the third one.

The third phrase (literally, "nor from the will of a husband") is understood by most commentators to indicate the generative power of an adult male, a husband. The NIV, NEB, and TEV use the phrase "husband's will" or "human father" to convey this.

The fourth prepositional phrase (literally, "out from God") declares the divine origin of regeneration. This is clear enough in the RSV, NASB, and NIV. The paraphrases in the NEB and TEV are not necessary. The NEB's translation was changed in the REB to "of God." And Newman and Nida, who normally defend the TEV, suggest that a better thought-for-thought translation would be "God himself caused them to be his children."[6]

1:14 And the Word became flesh and dwelt ["lived" in the NRSV] among us, full of

grace and truth; we have beheld his glory,
glory as of the only Son from the Father.
(RSV)

And the Word became flesh, and dwelt
among us, and we beheld His glory, glory
as of the only begotten from the Father, full
of grace and truth. (NASB)

The Word became flesh and lived for awhile
 (1st ed.) ["made his dwelling," 2d ed.]
among us. We have seen his glory, the glory
of the One and Only, who came from the
Father, full of grace and truth. (NIV)

So the Word became flesh; he came to
dwell among us, and we saw his glory,
such glory as befits the Father's only Son,
full of grace and truth. (NEB)

The Word became a human being and, full
of grace and truth, lived among us. We saw
his glory, the glory which he received as
the Father's only Son. (TEV)

All the versions with the exception of the TEV read,
"The Word became flesh." As this is a unique asser-
tion of the Son of God's incarnation, it must be

translated accurately. Fortunately, all the versions advance beyond the KJV's rendering, "was made," for this expression does not correctly translate the meaning of the Greek verb *egeneto,* which denotes the beginning of a new existence. The Word, who was God, became that which he had never been before—a man. When John says, "The Word became flesh," he must mean "The Word became a human being" (as in the TEV).[7] But this could imply that the Word, a divine person, assumed the personality of another, whereas the orthodox understanding of the incarnation is that the Word took on human nature (signified by the word "flesh"). Furthermore, it should be noted that John probably avoided the Greek word *anthropos* (man) and instead used *sarx* (flesh) because he was battling against a Docetic heresy. The Docetists, a gnostic sect, believed that flesh was evil; therefore, they taught that the Son of God did not possess real flesh but only the guise of it. John wanted to make it unquestionably clear that the Word partook of actual flesh. This historical background is critical for the proper exegesis and translation of this passage. Therefore, though it is linguistically appropriate to equate "flesh" with "man" or with "human being," it is theologically inaccurate. A safer way for the TEV to translate this expression might be, "The Word became human."

In the second clause of verse 14 (literally, "and tabernacled [or "pitched his tent"] in our midst"), all the translators chose not to translate the Greek verb *eskenosen* literally because "tabernacled" sounds foreign to the English ear. Among the five translations, three chose "dwelt" (RSV, NASB, NEB) and two selected "lived" (TEV, so also NRSV) or "lived for a while" (NIV, 1st ed.). Although these adaptations may accommodate the English reader, they eclipse a word that was pregnant with meaning to the original readers. As a case in point, here is precisely where dynamic equivalence fails. While the average modern reader would probably be perplexed if he read "tabernacled," the ancient reader of this Gospel, when hearing *eskenosen*, would associate it with the Old Testament tabernacle. In the Old Testament account, God dwelt among his people, Israel, by tabernacling among them in a tent. His presence and Shekinah glory filled that tabernacle; and wherever that tabernacle went in the journeys of Israel, God would also go (see Exodus 40). With this image in view, the writer, John, must have intended his readers to see the connection with the Old Testament tabernacle. If "tabernacled" (or "pitched his tent") is too peculiar to appear in the text of a translation, it should at least appear as a marginal reading accompanied by some explanation. And, finally, it should be pointed out that "made his dwelling" in the second edition of the NIV is much better than "lived for a while" (1st ed.), which captures only the transitory aspect of tabernacling while neglecting the act of dwelling.[8]

Before examining the next phrase ("we beheld his glory") and that which follows, we must note that among the versions there has been some rearrangement of the word order in the last part of verse 14. This is due to different interpretations of the grammatical identification of the Greek word *pleres* (full). As this word is often indeclinable, it could agree with the Greek words for "only Son" or "his glory" or "Word." Since its connection with "the Word" is more natural and suitable to the context (see 1:16), the RSV repositions the clause "full of grace and truth" to follow immediately its logical antecedent, "the Word." This rearrangement or word order, however, separates the compounded idea of tabernacling and beholding his glory—which is definitely evident in the Greek text. The NEB handles it better, by keeping the last clause in its proper position and then clarifying its antecedent, "the Father's only Son, full of grace and truth." The TEV aligns "full of grace and truth" with "his glory." The other two versions (NASB and NIV) retain the same syntax as in the Greek and, unfortunately, give the impression that "full of grace and truth" modifies "Father."

All the versions concur here (and in 1:16a, 17) as to the translation of *charis* (grace). The NIV and TEV, however, employ the word "blessing" in 1:16b (see discussion there). Here and in 1:17 *aletheia* uniformly becomes "truth." Yet, as Barclay Newman intimates, readers should not be surprised to see new versions changing "truth" to "reality"[9] According to John's special terminology, *aletheia* does not, in all instances, simply mean "truth" (as versus falsehood) or "veracity." It more often signifies "divine reality revealed."[10]

The last segment of this verse to be examined is: "We beheld his glory, glory as of the only Son from the Father" (RSV). Beginning with verse 14, John introduces a testimony on behalf of the eyewitnesses of Jesus (see also 1 John 1:1-3). He declares, "We beheld his glory." The Greek verb he uses (*etheasametha*) means more than "to see"; it means "to view, to gaze upon" ("theater" is an English derivative). Then John characterizes the glory that was seen as being special in that it belonged to one who possessed a unique relationship with the Father; that is, it was the glory of an only Son.

The Greek word underlying "only Son" is *monogenous,* which is derived from *monos* (only) and *genos* (kind, offspring). This word does convey the idea of birth but probably not as much as it emphasizes the notion of uniqueness. Therefore, the rendering "only begotten" can be misleading, for inherent in this term is the implication of generation—and much debate was incited in the early days of the church over how the Son was generated from the Father. It is better that the idea of generation be avoided in translation, as is done in the second edition of the NIV: "the One and Only."

The rendering "only begotten" probably originated from Jerome's Latin translation when Jerome changed *unicus* (unique) to *unigenitus* (only begotten). Prior to Jerome's translation, the old Latin Codex Vercellensis (A.D. 365) had translated *monogenous*, as *unicus*. The rendering "only begotten" was carried over to the KJV, then to the RV and ASV, and on to several twentieth century versions, including the NASB. Fortunately, the phrase has been adjusted in Weymouth, Moffatt, Goodspeed, Williams, and the other four more recent versions (RSV, NIV, NEB, TEV).

This "one and only Son," according to the original, came from the Father. The NIV makes this explicit, while the NEB and TEV say the glory came from the Father. But the Greek text does not indicate that the glory came from the Father to the Son (as in the NEB, TEV). Having just declared the incarnation of the Word, John is here viewing the Son as having come from the Father.

1:15 (John bore witness to him, and cried, "This was he of whom I said, 'He who comes after me ranks before me, for he was before me.'") (RSV)

John bore witness of Him, and cried out, saying, "This was He of whom I said, 'He who comes after me has a higher rank than I, for He existed before me.'" (NASB)

John testifies concerning him. He cries out, saying, "This was he of whom I said, 'He who comes after me has surpassed me because he was before me.'" (NIV)

Here is John's testimony to him: he cried aloud, "This is the man I meant when I said, 'He comes after me, but takes rank before me'; for before I was born, he already was." (NEB)

John spoke about him. He cried out, "This is the one I was talking about when I said, 'He comes after me, but he is greater than I am, because he existed before I was born.'" (TEV)

Following his own personal testimony, John (the evangelist) quotes the witness that John the Baptist made

on the day he baptized Jesus (see 1:30). On one
hand, this verse appears to interrupt the continuity
between verses 14 and 16; as such, it is parenthetical
in the RSV and a separate paragraph in the TEV and
NIV. But, on the other hand, verse 15 seems to substantiate sequentially the testimony of 1:1-14, inas-
much as the Baptist's declaration refers to both the
Word's eternal preexistence and incarnation, except
in reverse order. At any rate, the message, as transmitted in all five translations, is essentially uniform in
accuracy. They all relate that while the incarnate
Word came after John chronologically, he surpassed
John (in rank) because he existed before him.

> **1:16** And from his fulness have we all received,
> grace upon grace. (RSV)
>
> For of His fulness we have all received, and
> grace upon grace. (NASB)
>
> From the fullness of his grace we have all
> received one blessing after another. (NIV)
>
> Out of his full store we have all received
> grace upon grace; (NEB)
>
> Out of the fullness of his grace he has
> blessed us all, giving us one blessing after
> another. (TEV)

131

The connection between 1:14 and 1:16 is obvious:
1:14 concludes with "full of grace and truth," and
1:16 begins with "because out of his fullness we
all received." The Greek word translated "fullness"
is *pleroma*. To Greek Christian readers, *pleroma*
was a special term with particular significance. New
Testament writers used it to describe the all-inclu-
sive, all-sufficient Christ (cf. Col. 2:9). The NEB's
rendering, "his full store," captures this idea. The
NIV and TEV, based on a different interpretation,
specify that the fullness is "the fullness of his
grace." They made the addition "of his grace" in
order to compensate for replacing the words "grace
upon grace" with "one blessing after another" in
the last part of this verse. This is an unfortunate sub-
stitution because it obscures the meaning of "grace
upon grace." This phrase does not mean that Christ
gives us one blessing after another (in the sense
that we keep getting good things); the expression
means that there is no end to the supply of grace
that comes from Christ's fullness. The phrase suggests constant replacement and replenishment:
"continual accessions of grace, new grace coming
upon and superseding the former."[11]

> **1:17** For the law was given through Moses;
> grace and truth came through Jesus Christ.
> (RSV, NIV)

For the Law was given through Moses;
grace and truth were realized through
Jesus Christ. (NASB)

for while the Law was given through
Moses, grace and truth came through Jesus
Christ. (NEB)

God gave the Law through Moses, but
grace and truth came through Jesus Christ.
(TEV)

In this verse, John distinguishes the New Testament
dispensation from that of the Old Testament. The
NEB adds "while" and the TEV "but" to make sure
the reader notices the contrast. While the Old Testament law was something "given" by God through
the agent, Moses, grace and truth "came" or "were
realized" through Jesus Christ. Since the Greek
word *egeneto* can mean "came" (see 1:6), "came
into being" (see 1:3, 10), or "became" (see 1:14),
the translators must decide which meaning is called
for in each given context. In this verse, "came" was
selected for four of the translations and "were realized" for one—namely, the NASB.

1:18 No one has ever seen God; the only Son
["God the only Son" in NRSV], who is in the

bosom of the Father ["close to the Father's heart" in NRSV], he has made him known. (RSV)

No one has ever seen God; but God's only Son, he who is nearest to the Father's heart, he has made him known. (NEB)

No man has seen God at any time; the only begotten God, who is in the bosom of the Father, He has explained Him. (NASB)

No one has ever seen God, but God the One and Only, who is at the Father's side, has made him known. (NIV)

No one has ever seen God. The only Son, who is the same as God and is at the Father's side, he has made him known. (TEV)

The difference between the wording "only Son" in the RSV and NEB and the wording "the only begotten God" in the NASB (or "God the only Son" in the NIV, or "the only Son, who is the same as God" in the TEV) comes from a significant variance among the Greek New Testament manuscripts. The translation in the RSV and NEB is based upon the reading *monogenes huios*; the other translations are based upon *monogenes theos*. The latter reading ("an only One, God") has the support of the earliest manuscripts (the Bodmer Papyri—P66 and P75, Codex Sinaiticus, Codex Vaticanus, Codex Ephraemi Rescriptus); later manuscripts (Codex Alexandrinus, the Freer Gospel, and many later witnesses) read, "the only begotten Son." The first reading is clearly the preferred reading because it is the most difficult of the two and best explains the origin of the variation. Scribes would not be inclined to change a common wording ("only begotten Son") to an uncommon wording ("an only begotten God"—which is a literal translation). The reading in all the earliest manuscripts indicates that Jesus is here called "God," as well as "the one and only." This perfectly corresponds to the first verse of the prologue, where the Word is called "God" and is shown as the Son living in intimate fellowship with the Father—literally, "in the bosom of the Father." Among the five translations, two translate this phrase nearly word for word (RSV, NASB), and three paraphrase it; and of these three, the rendering "at the Father's side" (NIV, TEV) is far less picturesque than the translation "nearest to the Father's heart" (NEB) and "close the Father's heart" (NRSV).

In the last clause of this verse is a Greek word, *exegesato,* that derives from the verb that means "to lead one through an explanation, to narrate." The English word *exegesis* is derived from this word. An exegesis in biblical studies means a detailed explanation of a Bible passage—literally "a leading through" a portion of Scripture. The Word is the one who leads men through a detailed explanation of God. To render the Greek verb "made him known" (as in all the versions except the NASB) is too general and not very impressive. And the reader may not see the intended connection with "the Word" in 1:1. Indeed, 1:18 is a mirror of 1:1, for both speak of the Son's intimate relationship with the Father, of his being God, and of his being the expression—the explanation—of God. The best translation of them all, then, is the one in the NASB because it explicitly says, "He has explained Him."

The Son of God, called "the Word," came among men to explain the invisible God. Had he not come, God would have remained unknown by us. But the Word, who is himself God and knows God the Father, came to earth as a man among men to provide us with a full, living explanation of divinity.

NOTES

[1] Edwin Abbott, *Johannine Grammar* (London: Adam and Charles Black, 1906), 274-75.

[2]See Matthew 13:56; 26:18; Mark 6:3; 14:49; 1 Corinthians 16:10; 2 Corinthians 5:8; and Galatians 1:18.

[3] F. F. Bruce in his book *The English Bible* (New York: Oxford University Press, 1970) says of this:

> The last clause of John 1:1 [in NEB] reads: "what God was, the Word was." Is this what the clause really means? Or have the translators perhaps been moved by an unconscious desire to give a rather different rendering from the Authorized Version? On reflection, this is probably excellent exegesis of the words literally rendered in the older versions as "the Word was God." (p. 245)

[4]*Webster's Third New International Dictionary,* unabridged, s.v. "receive."

[5]Barclay Newman and Eugene Nida, *Translator's Handbook on the Gospel of John* (New York: United Bible Societies, 1980), 20.

[6]Ibid., 20.

[7]In *The Gospel According to St. John: With the Greek Text* (London: John Murray, 1908), B. F. Westcott defined *flesh* as follows:

> *Flesh* expresses here human nature as a whole regarded under its aspect of its present corporal embodiment, including of necessity the "soul" (12:27) and the spirit (11:33; 13:21) as belonging to the totality of man. (p. 11)

[8]In *Christianity Today* (28 Sept. 1973), F. F. Bruce criticized the NIV for failing to capture the meaning of *eskenosen*:

> In verse 14 the verb *eskenosen*, instead of being treated as an ingressive aorist, is rendered as though it were an imperfect: "The Word lived for a while among us." The phrase "for a while" is probably intended to bring out the idea of a temporary encampment in the verb *skenoo*. But why not retain the ingressive force by some such rendering as: "took up his temporary abode among us"? If a rendering of this verb in the present context, without becoming clumsy, could convey something of the shekinah idea also, that would be a further improvement. (p. 26)

The second edition of the NIV has a correction: "The Word became flesh and made his dwelling among us."

[9]Newman and Nida, *Handbook,* 653–55.

[10]In the *Theological Dictionary of the New Testament, vol. 1,* ed. Gerhard Kittel; trans. G. Bromiley (Grand Rapids, Mich.: Eerdmans, 1964), Rudolf Bultmann wrote:

In John *aletheia* denotes "divine reality" with reference to the fact (1) that this is different from the reality in which man first finds himself, and by which he is controlled, and (2) that it discloses itself and is thus revelation. (p. 245)

Newman and Nida (*Handbook*, 654) said that *aletheia* "is used of Ultimate Reality, of God who is real."

[11]Henry Alford, *The Greek Testament*, vol. 2 (1852; reprint, Grand Rapids, Mich.: Guardian Press, 1976), 1688.

APPENDIX

CHILDREN'S BIBLES

In recent years, major Bible publishers have been producing Children's Bibles. Most of these Bibles, however, do not have a Bible translation that was made specifically for children. Rather, many of the Children's Bibles have adult translations with artwork for children. Other Christian publishers have released so-called Children's Bibles that are nothing more than stories from the Bible accompanied by artwork. These Bible storybooks are not Bibles for children per se because they do not contain the entire Bible text and because the stories are not actual translations from the Bible.

A few publishers have taken existing Bible translations and simplified them for children. This was done for the Children's Version, which is a simplification and modernization of the King James Version. A more extensive simplification and revision process went into *The Bible for Children,* now displaying the *Simplified Living Bible* text. The latter is far more suitable for children than the former because *The Living Bible* was originally made for children and the new

Simplified Living Bible text was designed for third graders to read.

In the past few decades, several translations were made specifically for young people and/or new readers. As was just mentioned, the original impetus behind *The Living Bible* was that Ken Taylor wanted to make the Bible understandable to his own children, who had struggled to understand the King James Version. J. B. Phillips had the same motivation. His London youth group in the church he pastored could not comprehend the Authorized King James Version. This prompted him to make a translation of the Pauline Epistles. Phillips, encouraged by C. S. Lewis and others, eventually completed the entire New Testament, now known as the *The New Testament in Modern English*. Phillips' paraphrase, as well as Taylor's paraphrase, became popular among millions of people of all ages. Nonetheless, both of these versions have given young people throughout the world an easy-to-read, comprehendible presentation of God's Word.

Other publishers (and organizations) have created new translations for new readers—which includes people learning English as a second language, people with language disabilities, and children. Three such translations are described below.

NEW LIFE VERSION

This translation, made by Gleason H. Ledyard, was first published as the *Children's New Testament*. While serving as missionaries in northern Canada, Ledyard and his wife, Kathryn, worked with Eskimos who were just starting to learn English. This experience created a desire within them to make an English translation for people learning English as a second language. After translating a few books and distributing them to various individuals, they were told that their translation was excellent for children. Thus, the Ledyard's continued their work, finishing first the New Testament and then the Old Testament. Using several existing translations, they produced the New Life Version, published by Christian Literature International.

The genius of the New Life Version's readability is that it has a limited vocabulary and simplification of difficult biblical terms. The version, which has sold more than 6 million copies, has been published in many editions and has been distributed worldwide—especially to those who are learning English as a second language. This version is the text of the *Precious Moments Children's Bible,* published by Baker Book House.

INTERNATIONAL CHILDREN'S BIBLE: NEW CENTURY VERSION

The New Century Version is a new translation of the original languages, published in two editions: one for children called the *International Children's Bible* and one for adults, first appearing in a New Testament edition called *The Word* and now available with the entire Bible text in an edition called *The Everyday Bible,* published by Sweet.

The World Bible Translation Center developed the New Century Version by using an existing translation specifically prepared for the deaf, which is unique in that it has a limited vocabulary, and then making a new rendition based on the latest edition of *Biblia Hebraica Stuttgartensia* for the Old Testament and the third edition of the United Bibles Societies' *Greek New Testament* for the New Testament. (The translation for the deaf was published as *New Testament for the Deaf,* Baker Book House.)

There is an emphasis on simplicity and clarity of expression in both the adult and children editions of the New Century Version. The children's edition, however, is stylistically more simplistic than the adults' edition. The translators of the New Century Version wanted to make "the language simple enough for children to read and understand for themselves" (from the Preface). Therefore, the translators used short, uncomplicated sentences as well as vocabulary appropriate for children on a third-grade instructional level.

CONTEMPORARY ENGLISH VERSION

Barclay Newman of the American Bible Society is the pioneer of a new translation for early youth. Working according to Eugene Nida's model of dynamic equivalence, Newman, in cooperation with other members of the American Bible Society, has been producing fresh translations of New Testament books based upon the United Bible Societies' *Greek New Testament* (3d, corrected ed.). To date, three portions of the New Testament have been published: *A Book about Jesus* (containing passages from the four Gospels), *Luke Tells the Good News about Jesus,* and *Good News Travels Fast: The Acts of the Apostles.* The entire New Testament is due to be published in 1991. Portions of the Old Testament have also been translated, such as *A Few Who Dared*; more portions will appear in the near future.

Other Living Books® Best-Sellers

ANSWERS by Josh McDowell and Don Stewart. In a question-and-answer format, the authors tackle sixty-five of the most-asked questions about the Bible, God, Jesus Christ, miracles, other religions, and creation. 07-0021-X $4.95.

BUILDING YOUR SELF-IMAGE by Josh McDowell. Here are practical answers to help you overcome your fears, anxieties, and lack of self-confidence. Learn how God's higher image of who you are can take root in your heart and mind. 07-1395-8 $4.95.

THE CHILD WITHIN by Mari Hanes. The author shares insights she gained from God's Word during her own pregnancy. She identifies areas of stress, offers concrete data about the birth process, and points to God's sure promises that he will "gently lead those that are with young." 07-0219-0 $3.95.

COME BEFORE WINTER AND SHARE MY HOPE by Charles R. Swindoll. A collection of brief vignettes offering hope and the assurance that adversity and despair are temporary setbacks we can overcome! 07-0477-0 $6.95.

DARE TO DISCIPLINE by James Dobson. A straightforward, plainly written discussion about building and maintaining parent/child relationships based upon love, respect, authority, and ultimate loyalty to God. 07-0522-X $4.95.

DR. DOBSON ANSWERS YOUR QUESTIONS by James Dobson. In this convenient reference book, renowned author Dr. James Dobson addresses heartfelt concerns on many topics including marital relationships, infant care, child discipline, home management, and others. 07-0580-7 $5.95.

JOHN, SON OF THUNDER by Ellen Gunderson Traylor. In this saga of adventure, romance, and discovery, travel with John—the disciple whom Jesus loved—down desert paths, through the courts of the Holy City, to the foot of the cross, as he leaves his luxury as a privileged son of Israel for the bitter hardship of his exile on Patmos. 07-1903-4 $5.95.

Other Living Books® Best-Sellers

LIFE IS TREMENDOUS! by Charlie "Tremendous" Jones. Believing that enthusiasm makes the difference, Jones shows how anyone can be happy, involved, relevant, productive, healthy, and secure in the midst of a high-pressure, commercialized society. 07-2184-5 $3.95.

LORD, COULD YOU HURRY A LITTLE? by Ruth Harms Calkin. These prayer-poems from the heart of a godly woman trace the inner workings of the heart, following the rhythms of the day and seasons of the year with expectation and love. 07-3816-0 $3.95.

LORD, I KEEP RUNNING BACK TO YOU by Ruth Harms Calkin. In prayer-poems tinged with wonder, joy, humanness, and questioning, the author speaks for all of us who are groping and learning together what it means to be God's child. 07-3819-5 $3.95.

MORE THAN A CARPENTER by Josh McDowell. A hard-hitting book for people who are skeptical about Jesus' deity, his resurrection, and his claim on their lives. 07-4552-3 $3.95.

MOUNTAINS OF SPICES by Hannah Hurnard. Here is an allegory comparing the nine spices mentioned in the Song of Solomon to the nine fruits of the Spirit. A story of the glory of surrender by the author of *Hinds' Feet on High Places*. 07-4611-2 $4.95.

NOW IS YOUR TIME TO WIN by Dave Dean. In this true-life story, Dean shares how he locked into seven principles that enabled him to bounce back from failure to success. Read about successful men and women—from sports and entertainment celebrities to the ordinary people next door—and discover how you too can bounce back from failure to success! 07-4727-5 $3.95.

RAINBOW COTTAGE by Grace Livingston Hill. Safe at last, Sheila tries to forget the horrors of the past, unaware that terror is about to close in on her again. 07-5731-0 $4.95

THE SECRET OF LOVING by Josh McDowell. McDowell explores the values and qualities that will help both the single and married reader to be the right person for someone else. 07-5845-5 $4.95

Other Living Books® Best-Sellers

THE STORY FROM THE BOOK. The full sweep of *The Book*'s contents in abridged, chronological form, giving the reader the "big picture" of the Bible. 07-6677-6 $4.95.

SUCCESS: THE GLENN BLAND METHOD by Glenn Bland. The author shows how to set goals and make plans that really work. His ingredients for success include spiritual, financial, educational, and recreational balances. 07-6689-X $4.95.

THROUGH GATES OF SPLENDOR by Elisabeth Elliott. This unforgettable story of five men who braved the Auca Indians has become one of the most famous missionary books of all times. 07-7151-6 $4.95.

WHAT WIVES WISH THEIR HUSBANDS KNEW ABOUT WOMEN by James Dobson. The best-selling author of *Dare to Discipline* and *The Strong-Willed Child* brings us this vital book that speaks to the unique emotional needs and aspirations of today's woman. An immensely practical, interesting guide. 07-7896-0 $4.95.

WHY YOU ACT THE WAY YOU DO by Tim LaHaye. Discover how your temperament affects your work, emotions, spiritual life, and relationships, and learn how to make improvements. 07-8212-7 $4.95.

You can find all of these Living Books at your local Christian bookstore. If they are unavailable, send check or money order for retail price plus $2.00 postage and handling (U.S. and territories only) to:

Tyndale Family Products, Box 448, Wheaton, IL 60189-448

Prices and availability subject to change without notice.

Please allow 4-6 weeks for delivery.